CULTURE SHOCK!

Vietnam

Claire Ellis

Graphic Arts Center Publishing Company
Portland, Oregon

In the same series

Australia	Israel	Singapore
Borneo	Italy	South Africa
Britain	Japan	Spain
Burma	Korea	Sri Lanka
Canada	Malaysia	Syria
China	Morocco	Taiwan
France	Nepal	Thailand
Hong Kong	Norway	USA
India	Pakistan	
Indonesia	Philippines	

Illustrations by TRIGG
Cover photographs from The Image Bank, Singapore

© 1995 Times Editions Pte Ltd

This book is published by special
arrangement with Times Editions Pte Ltd
Times Centre, 1 New Industrial Road, Singapore 1953
International Standard Book Number 1-55868-242-2
Library of Congress Catalog Number 95-75926
Graphic Arts Center Publishing Company
P.O. Box 10306 • Portland, Oregon 97210 • (503) 226-2402

Printed in Singapore

CONTENTS

INTRODUCTION

Vietnam is a complex country that is changing fast and it can be a difficult place for a new arrival to adjust to. This book has been designed to help both short- and long-term visitors to Vietnam. Understanding the Vietnamese people, their way of life and their culture will mean your time in the country is far easier, more enjoyable and, particularly for the business person, more profitable. The country has been strongly influenced by the Chinese but do not make the mistake of thinking that its cultural ways are the same, an error the Vietnamese will not thank you for. For individuals and families who settle in the country, reading about the concept of culture shock and understanding its probable impact on you, as well as on others around you, helps you make the mental adjustments necessary to succeed and be happy in Vietnam.

Vietnam has a long, war-torn history and is physically an elongated, beautiful and diverse country. Both the history and geography have had a dramatic impact on the people. There are significant differences across generations and between provinces. The first two chapters help provide this information and cannot be ignored as background if you want to understand Vietnam as it is today.

Currently, the country is in a state of flux, moving from a closed communist system to one incorporating laissez-faire ideas and welcoming international visitors. For information on current rules and regulations, it is essential that you seek alternative sources. This book contains a bibliography that will help point you in the right direction for this information as well as for further reading on a variety of other topics.

ACKNOWLEDGEMENTS

The culture of the Vietnamese people of today is a topic that is little written about. Much of the information gathered in this book was developed not just from living and experiencing the people and the country myself, but also from hundreds of interviews with people from different walks of life throughout the country, both Vietnamese and foreign.

My gratitude goes to all who gave their time, knowledge and experience freely to help see this information collated into one place and bring the book to completion. I am particularly thankful to the people in business who related problems or incidents that had occurred in their company, trusting me not to break the confidential aspects of the information, and to the Vietnamese who spoke of their experiences dealing with foreigners and who shared their customs with me, some still strongly adhered to, others disappearing slowly.

Special mention must go to Lydia Snape for her tireless help in adding to the content and improving the grammar and structure and to my husband, Anthony Ellis, who took most of the photographs.

Claire Ellis

LANGUAGE NOTES

Chapter 6, on Communication, discusses the language, its alphabet and correct pronunciation in detail. However, as this book is designed for non-Vietnamese readers, some liberties have been taken with the use of Vietnamese in the remaining text. This is to make it easier and quicker to read.

The Vietnamese alphabet includes a number of diacritical symbols that designate how a word should be pronounced, or that are used to denote different vowel and consonant sounds. One word can have several meanings and without these additional diacritics, the meaning of a word can be ambiguous. For a non-Vietnamese, however, these extra symbols can be confusing and make reading difficult. In the general text of this book, the sentence clarifies the Vietnamese word so no diacritics are used.

In most cases, place names and people's names are spelt according to Vietnamese custom (diacritics omitted) but the better-known places are spelt according to English custom. Hence, Hanoi is written as one word rather than as Ha Noi. Similarly, the more common geographical terms are used so we have, for instance, the Mekong River instead of its Vietnamese name of Cuu Long River, and the Spratly Islands instead of Quan Dao Thruong Xa, as the islands are called in Vietnamese.

It is hoped that these variations do not lead to inaccuracies or confuse the reader, but simply speed reading comprehension.

Chapter One

VIETNAM – THE COUNTRY

The land and sea that form the country of Vietnam have played an integral role in the development of its people. A land border is shared with China, Laos and Cambodia and this central position in East Asia has shaped the country's war-torn history. Tropical forests, mangrove swamps, fertile plains and long beaches; a climate that varies greatly from north to south, and season to season; and a wealth of natural resources all exist here. They have influenced the Vietnamese way of life and made the country what it is today.

A glance at a map shows Vietnam stretching 1,650 km from north to south, although a mere 600 km at its widest and just over 50 km at its narrowest. Three-quarters of the land is mountainous but the other quarter consists of rich alluvial plains where most of the people live. The country is shaped like an "S" as it winds its way down the length of the Indo-Chinese peninsula, its southern coast overlooking the South China Sea. Many writers have likened the shape to a peasant carrying a bamboo pole, with a large rice basket on either end.

Vietnam is divided into three geographical regions—the south, centre and north. The massive Mekong (Cuu Long) River in the south and the Red River in the north are the principal agricultural areas where most of the population live. They are the "rice bowls" of the country. The thin, central strip separating them is the "bamboo pole".

This physical separation has had a lasting impact on the country's history and, therefore, on the people. Despite now being one unified nation, there are clear cultural differences between the people of the south, centre and north, due in part to the geography of the land.

Its land mass of 330,363 sq km is only a small part of its total territory, since it also claims a large sea area from the Tonkin Gulf to the Gulf of Thailand. This region is approximately three times the size of the land area of Vietnam. Over 1,000 small islands lie within the zone and these, together with the country's long coastline, prime trading position, navigable rivers and reliance on fishing for food, mean that boating traditions are strong and water transport is vital in many areas. However, Vietnam's marine claims are in part disputed by its neighbours. The Paracel Islands are also claimed by China and the Spratly Islands, closer to Borneo, are claimed by Malaysia, Brunei, the Philippines, Taiwan and China as well.

The South

This region was called Cochin-China (Bac Ky) by the French but is now known as Nam Bo. It is distinctly different from the north. The climate is tropical and the land is rich. The people have not had to work very hard to make a living and so are seen as lazy by many. While in the north, farmers tend to work communal land, here in the south, more are owners and they also engage in selling or bartering excess produce. Throughout history, the southern region has been influenced primarily by the Khmers (people of a kingdom in Cambodia founded in A.D. 435) and not the Chinese, as in the north.

Southern Vietnam is dominated by the passage of the Mekong River through it. Meandering 4,500 km from its source in eastern Tibet, it flows through China, Burma, Laos, Thailand and Cambodia before emptying into the South China Sea in southern Vietnam. The river provides vital irrigation water for thousands of paddy fields along the way and its muddy discharge brings rich alluvial soil that fertilises and replenishes the ground. As the sediment settles out on reaching the sea, the delta grows and extends the country eastwards by approximately 75 metres annually. The result is a vast maze of water channels making up a delta that covers 60,000 sq km. These were conducive to the growth of the strong trading empires of the past.

Ho Chi Minh City

Ho Chi Minh City, the new name for Saigon, lies just to the north of this delta, about half a day's drive away. It is the largest city in Vietnam and functions as its economic heart and business hub, with 30% of the country's manufacturing and 25% of its retail trade carried out here. It has a population of about four million, but this is still a small proportion of the total of 72 million inhabitants in the country.

To understand its current trading pre-eminence, one will have to look into the past. Saigon, the name of the original town, has always been a commercial city and a regional centre. Situated on the coast, the region became an important link between India and China from the first to the sixth centuries A.D. It started as a Khmer trading post but it was not until the 17th and 18th centuries that it consolidated its regional position and started its dramatic expansion.

Historically, the city's geographical position has helped it to establish its economic dominance. Until recently, half of Vietnam's export earnings came from just two products: rice and crude oil.

The mighty Mekong delta, Vietnam's greatest rice-producing area, lies just to the south of Ho Chi Minh City. Over time, the country's production has risen dramatically from scarcely being able to provide for its own population to being among the world's top three rice exporters. As for crude oil, much of it lies off the coast, east of nearby Vung Tau.

Booming trade is now evident as Ho Chi Minh City continues to expand rapidly and cement its position as the economic capital of Vietnam. A study by the General Statistics Office done in 1992 shows that the per capita income in Ho Chi Minh City and its surrounding provinces is 2.7 times higher than the national average. This area is followed by Hanoi and the Mekong delta, which have an income that is 116–126% of the national average. The population of Ho Chi Minh City grows every day. Foreign businessmen come and people flock in from rural areas, all hoping to benefit from its growing economy. This action is starting to cause major infrastructural problems.

Vung Tau

Vung Tau lies 128 km away on the delta of the Saigon River and was known previously by its French name of Cap Saint Jacques, it was the place where American soldiers enjoyed their rest and recreation (R&R) breaks. To the latest set of foreign visitors, however, it is known as a new oil frontier town. It remains popular as a seaside resort and the beaches are packed on weekends, when both locals and foreigners living in Ho Chi Minh City come down for a break in the sun. It is the main servicing point for the country's offshore oil fields. Gas reserves are also waiting to be exploited and while there may not be sufficient amounts to create a long-term export industry, they are being harnessed for the fuel needs of the south.

The Mekong Delta

Further south flows the life-blood of the region. This huge river may appear unimpressive at first sight as, in the delta region, it is impossible to see the size of the whole river. The Mekong divides into two at Phnom Penh in Cambodia, where it forms the Hau Giang, or Bassac River, and the Tien Giang, or Upper River. The former subsequently divides into three and flows into the South China Sea at Chau Doc, Long Xuyen and Can Tho. The Upper River then splits into another six. It spreads out to cover a massive expanse and the people of the delta live along the rivers in houseboats or in stilt houses. Taking a boat through the network of canals is the main means of transport as many areas do not have roads.

This maze of canals was one of the last places the Viet Cong fighters of the north conquered as they moved south. It was known as a refuge for pirates, religious apostates, political exiles, smugglers and anyone involved in underground operations. On a less clandestine note, it is also known for the incredible variety of agricultural products it produces, including rice, maize, beans, peas, sugar, sesame, potatoes, melons, pumpkins, eggplants and cabbage, as well as fish, frogs, snakes, turtles, limestone and medicinal products.

My Tho is the principal town on the northern side and is the usual entrance to the region from Ho Chi Minh City. But Can Tho is the capital of Hau Giang province, which covers most of the delta, and so is the region's centre. It has a university with one of the biggest agronomy departments in the country. Long Xuyen is slightly smaller than Can Tho and is the other major town within the delta, being the capital of the An Giang province. It is best known as the centre for the Hoa Hao religious sect that, until 1956, had its own army.

As one moves further south and west, the Thai and Cambodian influence strengthens and more goods from these countries are available. The town of Ca Mau lies on the southern tip of Vietnam within a vast mangrove swamp, called the U-Minh forest, covering over 1,000 sq km. It is the largest mangrove swamp outside the Amazon Basin but, unfortunately, suffered vast defoliation during the Vietnam War. Despite re-planting, over 20% of the area is still considered to be wasteland.

Ecologically, it is of prime importance as it is the breeding place of many varieties of shrimp and fish, as well as birds. The Tram Chim Crane Reserve was established to help protect the breeding site of the red-necked crane, which returned to breed again in 1986, after the disruptions of the Vietnam War. The region supports the lowest population density in southern Vietnam and includes many ethnic Khmers. They make a living from fishing and the mangrove trees that provide tannin, thatch, timber and charcoal. During the flowering season, there is abundant food for bees, so honey and beeswax are additional sources of revenue.

Rounding the southernmost tip of Vietnam and moving east towards Cambodia, the land now lies against the Gulf of Thailand. Rach Gia is the capital of Kien Giang province and close to it lie the remains of Oc-Eo, the capital of the Funan kingdom of the first to sixth centuries. In a politically sensitive zone only 8 km from the Cambodian border is the town of Ha Tien, an area well-known for its lovely white beaches and its production of black pepper, seafood and turtle products. The drop-shaped island of Phu Quoc, an idyllic tropical island with beautiful beaches and a mountainous, forested interior, is 45 km from Ha Tien. It is best known for its production of high quality *nuoc mam,* the Vietnamese fish sauce.

Da Lat

Inland and north from Ho Chi Minh City lies the scenic hill town of Da Lat. It takes approximately five hours by car to get there and the journey is fascinating. Churches abound just outside of Ho Chi Minh City as the area was settled by Christians who had fled south in 1954, after the establishment of the communist regime in the north. Some of the newer churches are said to have been financed by Vietnamese now living overseas. Moving up into the hills towards Da Lat, the flatter regions grow vegetables, tobacco, sugarcane, flowers such as gladioli and roses, strawberries and acres and acres of mulberries to keep the silkworms alive in the nearby factories.

The people of Da Lat wear thick clothing to protect themselves against the cold mountain air.

As the temperature drops 0.5°C with every 100 m of elevation, Da Lat is pleasantly cool at approximately 1,500 m above sea level. In the past, the emperors reserved land here as hunting estates, their favourite targets being the elephant, tiger and gaur. In fact, tiger-hunting remained popular up to the late 1950s. Da Lat taxidermists are famous and their work continues to be in demand. Now, the region is more popular as a destination for honeymooners and forested areas still exist in the more precipitous zones. Such areas often have cascading waterfalls.

Da Lat itself is surrounded by vast pine forests that are tapped for resin. Unlike most of Vietnam, it emerged relatively unscathed from the Vietnam War. It is said that leaders from both sides used the area as a recreational base to escape the heat and there was a mutual understanding to leave the zone alone. Whether this account is true or not, the area did escape the bombing raids that destroyed other towns.

The Coastal Strip

The narrow coastal strip that heads north from Ho Chi Minh City is dotted with many tiny fishing villages and the occasional larger town. This region tends to be quite dry and agriculture is poor, unless there are rivers allowing irrigation through the dry season. The people turn to the sea for their livelihood and fish, prawns, squid and the making of *nuoc mam* are the major sources of income. The in-shore waters are now becoming quite over-fished. In desperation, some people have used techniques such as dynamite fishing to improve the size of their catch. Such short-sighted action has unpleasant long-term effects. It destroys the shallow coral reefs and has led to even further degradation of the fish population.

Highway One links the small towns together and the first major one heading north is Phan Thiet, known for its *nuoc mam* and fish. Despite being semi-arid, the area has excellent grapes and trellises and vines can be seen around many of the houses. Following the coastline, Cam Ranh Bay was a port favoured by the Russians during the Russo-Japanese War, by the Japanese during World War II, by the Americans during the Vietnam War and by the Russians again after 1975. The beaches here are beautiful but a little further north, the beaches of Nha Trang attract a great deal more tourists. As the capital of Khanh Hoa province, Nha Trang is one of the larger towns, having a population of over 250,000. Numerous offshore islands make great day-trip destinations for fishermen or snorkellers and the country's premier Oceanographic Institute is located here. While tourism is a growing industry and old French villas along the beach front are receiving face lifts, fishing remains the primary source of income. Other income earners are cashew nuts, coffee, salt, sesame seeds and coconuts.

Continuing past Qui Nhon and Quang Ngai city, Da Nang is the country's fourth largest city, with a population of over 500,000. It was the most important port in central Vietnam and had the French name of Tourane in the last century. Vietnam's political structure allows for a high degree of autonomy and the Da Nang leaders have made the most of their proximity to both Laos and Thailand. As Laos is landlocked, Da Nang is the main port for South Laos, and foreign investment and economic progress are welcomed in the city. Because of this, the area seems quite dynamic compared with many of its compatriot coastal towns.

The natural landscape surrounding Da Nang is spectacular and China Beach, stretching for many miles, has been the site of an international surfing competition and was formerly a popular R&R spot for American troops. Just inland, the Marble Mountains consist of five stone hills, each of which has special significance. The largest has many caves that were once used by the Chams (people of the Champa kingdom that emerged in central Vietnam in the second century) to worship their Hindu gods. Later, they were used by the Buddhists and by communist insurgents of the north to bombard the U.S. army base of China Beach during the Vietnam War. Today, the Vietnamese travel from all over the country to visit these shrines and enjoy the sights.

Impressive scenery is created when the mountain range meets the sea, such as at Hai Van Pass (Pass of the Clouds) between Hue and Da Nang. Until the 11th century, this natural border marked the traditional boundary between the Viets (people of the Viet tribe) in the north and the Chams on the southern side. The French used it to delineate Annam from Tonkin and now it acts as the border between Quang Binh and Nghe Tinh provinces.

Hue, with 250,000 people, was the nation's capital during the Nguyen dynasty from 1802 to 1945. It is known as one of the country's cultural, religious and educational centres but many important buildings and items were destroyed either during the sacking of the city by the French in 1885, or many years later when the Americans fought to regain the city from the communists during the 1968 Tet Offensive. Luckily some of the beautiful buildings still remain and the Imperial City is slowly being restored with help from UNESCO. The Perfume River flows through the city, which is equally famous for its good food and beautiful girls.

Hoi An was a major international port during the 17th to 19th centuries and from here, sailors travelled as far as Thailand and Indonesia while ships of Portuguese, Dutch, Spanish, Indian, Arab, Filipino, Thai, French, American, Chinese and Japanese nationalities used to dock for trading. Archaeological excavations show that the town has been inhabited for at least 2,200 years and was an important centre for high-grade silk. It was the first point where Christianity entered Vietnam and also the first site where ethnic Chinese settled in southern Vietnam. Here, more so than in other parts of the country, the Chinese are well assimilated with the Vietnamese and most of them rarely speak their native tongue now. The city, now the home of 55,000 people, suffered little damage during the numerous wars that ravaged the country, so excellent architectural features reflecting much of its past trading history can still be seen.

All through this central coastal region from Phan Thiet northwards to Deo Ngang on the 18th parallel, evidence of the majestic Champa empire (2nd to 14th century A.D.) can be seen. Ruined temples and towers remain scattered throughout the countryside. Their distinctive Hindu shapes clearly demonstrate their origins and many descendants of the Chams still live in this region. They cultivate relatively large fields and use a special hydraulic system to interconnect canals and ponds. Their methods of pottery, fishing, sugar production, silk-making and construction all reflect a cultural heritage that is different from that of the Vietnamese.

As you travel north, you will cross the Ben Hai River, the line that split the country in two from 1954 to 1975. The demilitarised zone had a 4 km buffer on either side. Nearby land and mountain tops were artificially levelled. The region was ruined by massive carpet bombing and the land has been permanently pock-marked with bomb craters. Even now, few plants grow in the ground and metal fragments provide the scrap merchants with a livelihood.

The Central Highlands

The narrow strip of central Vietnam has the Truong Son mountain range (formerly called the Annamite Cordillera) running in a north-south direction and providing the physical barrier between Vietnam and Laos. High plateaus squeeze most of the population onto the thin coastal strip of central Vietnam, but the highlands have rich volcanic soil and are valuable coffee, tea and timber areas.

The topography allows for few roads so the region remains relatively untouched and poorly populated. Here, a varied ethnic mix consisting of hill tribes can be found. The majority live a subsistence way of life practising slash-and-burn agriculture although it is becoming increasingly untenable for many. While more difficult to travel through, the area is interesting as traditional costumes and customs, such as long-stemmed pipe-smoking by the women, can still be seen.

A few areas are accessible and fertile. Buon Me Thuot, just north of Da Lat and the capital of the Dac Lac province, has a population of over 65,000 and much of its industry is based on the region's extensive coffee plantations initially set up by the French. Further north, the principal towns are Pleiku and Kontum, lying on a broad plateau of fertile volcanic soil. The caves at Phong Nha, northwest of Dong Hoi, are filled with stalactites and stalagmites which have created a natural attraction over the centuries.

Vinh is the capital of the Nghe Tinh province, one of Vietnam's poorest regions suffering from infertile soil, a harsh climate and frequent typhoons. Life is tough for the people and the area suffered extensively during the French and Vietnam wars. These factors may have helped develop a strong spirit of revolutionary freedom and the province is the birthplace of people influential in Vietnam's recent history, such as Ho Chi Minh and Phan Boi Chau.

The North

North Vietnam (Bac Bo), or Tonkin as it was called by the French, has spectacular scenery and is said to be the most beautiful part of Vietnam. High mountain chains separate China from north Vietnam, with the highest peak of Phan Si Pan rising 3,143 m. These mountain chains helped protect the Vietnamese population from the stronger Chinese dynasties in early history. The Red River starts in China's Yunnan province and flows 400 km to the sea, creating a fertile delta that was the cradle of the Vietnamese civilisation. It spreads over 15,000 sq km but, unlike the much larger Mekong delta, the Red River delta floods regularly.

Hanoi, the nation's capital, dominates the region and lies on the banks of the Red River. It is the political, cultural and educational capital of the country, but is not as large as Ho Chi Minh City, having only three million inhabitants. The recent economic boom fuelled by foreign currency has been centred on the south and the north is quieter, the pace less frenetic. The expatriate population tends to be dominated by the presence of the diplomatic groups, but is starting to expand as more businesses are located there, complying with the government's wishes to distribute more evenly the location of wealth throughout the country.

The city has preserved much of the past both physically and mentally. The Hoan Kiem Lake (Lake of the Restored Sword or Small Lake) is surrounded on the east and south side by lovely old French-style buildings and tree-lined avenues. From the north shore runs the old quarter with streets specialising in different products. The people are polite and much more reserved than the brasher southerners. Hospitality is still very gracious. The region has been inhabited since neolithic times and became a capital when Emperor Ly Thai To established it in 1010. Shortly afterwards, in 1070, the first Temple of Literature was established there (and can still be visited) and by 1076, a university was built to educate the sons of the wealthy. The name "Hanoi", given to it by Emperor Tu Duc in 1831, means "City on a Bend in the River".

Typical street scene in the capital city of Hanoi.

Hanoi is one of the most charming cities in Vietnam and the government is looking for ways to preserve its architecture and unique blend of history while also allowing modern offices, hotels and general expansion. There are several smaller lakes in the city and central Hanoi is divided into four districts, although Greater Hanoi spreads over a much larger area.

Looking east, Ha Long Bay covers an area of over 1,500 sq km, containing more than 3,000 limestone islands that appear to climb vertically from the sea. They are as popular now for tourists as they were as hideaways for pirates in the past. Nearby Haiphong is the country's third largest city of 1.5 million, and the main industrial region and port for the north. It played an important role in keeping Soviet and Chinese supplies from reaching North Vietnamese troops during the Vietnam War.

Further north of Hanoi lie the mountains that separate China from Vietnam. Sparsely populated by a few hill tribes, the region is made attractive by spectacular waterfalls and deep valleys carpeted with jungle. But there are few roads because of the rough terrain and the border region is still a sensitive zone. The country's first and best-preserved national park, Cuc Phuong, lies 100 km southwest of Hanoi. It was established in 1962 and provides a haven for many of the rare species of animals that inhabit the forests. There are few major towns here except for Dien Bien Phu, site of the famous battle that forced the French to withdraw from Vietnam, and also Son La, lying on the traditional caravan route from Burma and China to Hanoi. Many fascinating ethnic groups still live in this region.

CLIMATE

Vietnam starts in the north at 23° 20' and its southernmost tip lies at 8° 33'. Consequently, the climate differs markedly depending on which part of the country you are in. The south is tropical, remaining hot all year. Ho Chi Minh City receives approximately 1,900 mm of rain a year, mostly in the wet season that stretches from May to October. The dry season is from November to April. The hottest months are March to May and temperatures can reach about 35°C. For the rest of the year, the temperature averages from 26° to 33°C.

The north, however, has a distinct summer and winter season, but remains humid. Hanoi's hottest period is from June to August, with an average maximum of 32°C in July. Winter stretches from November to April and the average temperature can drop to 10°C on a cold January night as polar winds sweep in from China. Generally, it is cool and pleasant although the temperature can fluctuate rather drastically. In the mountains, it drops below freezing point. The average rainfall is 1,600 mm a year, peaking in August.

Summer monsoons between August and November affect the length of coastal Vietnam and during this time, the humidity is recorded at 80–85%. Typhoons swing in from the sea and as they hit the coast, they usually bring heavy rain and can cause a great deal of destruction. This is a popular time to visit towns higher in the mountains, where the temperature drops to a pleasant level overnight and the rain and high humidity of the coastal region can be avoided.

POPULATION

Vietnam's population of 72 million is far from evenly distributed. The majority live on the flat plains along the country's coastal strip, particularly in the delta of the Red River and Mekong River, while the inland mountains remain sparsely populated. Just below 30% of Vietnam's land is used for agriculture. Over 60% of the population still live off the land and many more lead a rural life in small villages, but there is a trend towards increased urbanisation. The largest city is Ho Chi Minh City, with a conservative estimated population of 4 million. Next is Hanoi (just over 3 million), followed by Haiphong (1.5 million), Da Nang (500,000) and Hue and Nha Trang (250,000).

Vietnam's population has been growing rapidly in recent years. It stood at six million in the 18th century, 13 million at the beginning of the 19th century and is now officially over 72 million, and probably closer to 74 million. Growth has been far from even and the 1945 famine saw a drop from 22 million to 20 million. During the more recent wars, over two million Vietnamese were estimated to have lost their lives. Life expectancy figures are low at 62 years for women and 58 years for men (1988). The male-female ratio is also badly skewed because of the wars.

The birth rate is high. Approximately 50% of the population is less than 20 years old, causing massive problems in the provision of education. As this group hits the workforce, it is hoped that the booming economy will be able to generate sufficient jobs for the increased supply of manpower. These youths were all born after the Vietnam War and, therefore, have never experienced the horrors that their parents lived through. There is an increasing mental divide between the young and the old because of this (see Chapter 3, The People).

NATURAL RESOURCES

Three-quarters of Vietnam was once covered with dense forests rich in natural resources such as high-quality timber, rattan, oil, resin and medicinal plants. Asiatic animals such as the Asian elephant, rhinoceros, tiger, bear, deer, monkeys and an enormous variety of birds, fish, reptiles and insect life proliferated. Unfortunately, the combination of a growing population and vast chemical deforestation during the Vietnam War has left the country devastated environmentally. Erosion and chemical residues meant vast areas of agricultural land were lost. Siltation ruined irrigation systems and hydro-electrical works and forest loss have altered weather patterns and caused flash flooding to occur.

Problems on such a large scale are proving very difficult to solve. The government has embarked on programmes for reforestation and the provision of water catchment zones. National Parks are also being set aside to help restore the ecological balance. Today, Vietnam has regained much of its agricultural land and is estimated to have over 273 mammal species, 773 bird species, 180 reptile species and 80 amphibians. Much of these have not been studied in detail and Vietnam is one of the few places in the world where new species of large mammals can still be discovered. In 1992, a primitive species of ox and, in 1994, a new species of deer were discovered at Vu Quang near the Laos border.

Vietnam is rich in a number of minerals particularly high-quality anthracite coal used for electricity, iron ore for steel and cast-iron, copper, lead-zinc, bauxite, apatite for phosphate fertilisers and some precious metals such as chromium, titanium, gold, tungsten and tin. It also has fine clay for the production of porcelain, gemstones, quartz sand and a growing oil and gas industry. Regions such as the northwest are believed to be rich in minerals but are as yet little explored. This may change soon as the government is looking into legally linking exploration and exploitation rights.

Agriculture has always been the cornerstone of the economy and Vietnam is the world's third largest rice exporter (after United States and Thailand). Rice is also the staple of most Vietnamese meals, supplemented by corn, cassava and sweet potato in the poorer areas. Rubber, tea and coffee are major exports from the highland regions and the forests provide bamboo, cinnamon, lacquer, resin, quinine and valuable timber. Pineapple, lychee, rambutan, banana, watermelon and mango proliferate. Fruit and vegetable canning are important industries for the local and export markets together with peanut, oilseed and animal husbandry (processed meat is a major export). Other important cash crops are coconut, pepper, tobacco, sugarcane, reed, jute, cotton and mulberry. Fisheries are also well developed with aqua-culture providing much of the fish and shrimp as well as the traditional products of fish sauce, fish paste, dried cuttlefish and dried fish.

Manufacturing industries are starting to expand as new money and technology allow them to become more competitive in the international market. Heavy industry is concentrated in the north with steel and cement plants, as well as food processing, canning and textile factories. The traditional areas of art and handicraft have long been successful and the textile and garment industries are well established in the production of cotton and silk. The country's main exports are rice, timber, coal, coffee, tea, rubber, processed meat and crude oil. Imports consist of oil products and fertilisers.

Tourism is increasing rapidly as the infrastructure improves and travelling becomes easier, but Vietnam's most valuable resource lies in its people. They provide a cheap labour force which is attracting new industries as the country's economy opens up. More importantly, the Vietnamese are receptive to new ideas and ways of doing things. Now that the country is at peace and able to benefit from overseas investments and technologies, its economy is expected to follow the growth path of its more successful Asian neighbours.

Chapter Two

VIETNAM –
HISTORICALLY AND TODAY

The Vietnamese have a wonderful analogy about themselves. They are like a country house with an open door located on each of its four walls. The wind can blow in from any direction and when it has abated, the house still stands and retains none of the wind. Invaders have come from many directions but, through it all, Vietnam has retained its own national characteristics.

HISTORY

Vietnam, as a single unified country, has not existed until recently. To talk of the people and to help understand present-day Vietnam and its complexities, we need to examine the history of the region and see how the country was forged. For centuries, the area was much fought over. There have been few periods of prolonged peace and even during these, Vietnam has been subjected to the influence of other nations because of its geographical location on the Indo-Chinese peninsula and in the centre of eastern Asia. A quick review of the people's struggles to form a country despite many wars and hardships shows their determination to achieve the long-term goals of independence and unity.

Vietnam's history is not simply an examination of the area and the struggles by various tribes and empires for dominance, but must also include the influences that have arrived from visitors. Situated along the coast of the Asian continent, Vietnam has always been an important stopover for Arab, Chinese, Indian and other trading nations. The early name for the region, Indo-China, reflected the important link that it provided between India and China. The name was given by the French and much of what is now known about the region comes from Western exploration of it. This began in the 16th century when French, Dutch and Portuguese missionaries visited the area to spread their gospel. But Vietnam's history goes back even further and it is these earlier times that have forged the country into what it is today.

Early historical accounts of Vietnam are usually written as the history of the group of people known as Viets, from the northern part of the country. Such accounts rarely include anything but a cursory description of the many other tribes that exist. Most of the present-day Vietnamese are descended from the Viet tribe, which eventually went on to conquer and unify the country. So it is Viet history that seems most important to the Vietnamese. The majority of the other tribes have never played an important role in the region's politics and have always been relatively small in numbers. Little is known of some of the other groups that once lived and flourished. The Chams, for instance, have a 2,000-year-old history based on large trading empires but the group has now vanished, having been absorbed into the Viet empire. Much of its culture is also lost.

Vietnam's history is intertwined with that of its neighbours Cambodia and, in particular, China. As the kingdoms and dynasties in the region waxed and waned, so did their influence on the Vietnamese empires. More recently, the global superpowers have also recognised the strategic position of Vietnam and, as a result, many people outside the country know more about the recent wars that have been fought there than of the people and their heritage.

Early History

Archaeological discoveries suggest that the presence of man in this region dates back to the Paleolithic era, 300,000–500,000 years ago, in the Ma River valley southwest of Hanoi. Primitive agriculture can be traced back to 9,000 years ago, and the descendants of today's Vietnamese made their appearance around the fourth millennium B.C.

Vietnamese legends, however, tell a far more picturesque story of the people's origin. There was once a lonely dragon (an ancient symbol of good luck and fortune) in China that wandered south and found a beautiful land. The dragon was personified as Kinh Duong Vuong who went to the Waters Palace, married the dragon lord's daughter and had a son, Lac Long Quan. Lac taught his subjects how to till, sow and prepare foods. He established an organised society and, in time, married an immortal princess named Au Co. She gave birth to a flesh-bag containing 100 eggs from which hatched 100 children. But there were now too many people in one place, so Lac and Au Co parted company. Fifty sons went with Au Co and settled in the mountains, near present-day Hanoi. The eldest son was elected king and he established the Hung dynasty, the first Vietnamese kingdom. It went on to prosper during the first millennium B.C. and covered much of northern Vietnam, and many of Vietnam's legends stem from this period. The other 50 sons stayed with their father, Lac, at the

Waters Palace on the South Sea. Once the children had grown, Lac and his wife were reunited in the spirit world. Hence, legend has it that the Vietnamese are descended from two potent symbols: a dragon lord, Lac, and an immortal princess, Au Co. More importantly, all Vietnamese are related to each other.

Many old traditions are said to have been passed down from Lac, the first king of Vietnam. For instance, he initiated the idea of painting eyes on the bows of boats. It is believed that the eyes are able to scare away sharks and other dangers, as well as help the fishermen find the best fishing spots and bring good luck.

An early name for Vietnam was Au Lac, reflecting the country's origins. From the Hung dynasty onwards, empires came and went depending on the strength of their rulers and that of their neighbours. The Au Lac dynasty followed the Hung dynasty and during this reign, the Dong Son culture flourished and spread, eventually influencing much of Southeast Asia, extending as far as the eastern islands of Indonesia. This culture is famous for its well-developed bronze work in which magnificent drums were forged and used for religious and ceremonial purposes. Today, the remains of a spiral citadel built during the Au Lac reign at the capital of Phuc An can be seen at the village of Co Loa, to the west of Hanoi. Wealth came from rich trade routes to the north and west. This was not a long-lived dynasty, however, due to increasing incursions from the Chinese to the north. As they found routes through the mountain chain that protects Vietnam from China, the proto-Vietnamese groups gradually inter-bred with those of southern China, resulting in the present-day racial mix.

Chinese Influence

Ten centuries of domination, first from the Han dynasty starting in the 2nd century B.C. and, later, the Tang dynasty, has left a firm imprint on the northern Vietnamese way of life. Even today, many celebrations and cultural practices appear to the visitor to be basically

Chinese in character. It is true that many innovations came from China but these have evolved over time to suit the Vietnamese way of life and many subtle differences between the two countries have emerged.

China was very advanced and the flow of knowledge and technology provided enormous benefits for Vietnam. New ways were rapidly accepted and improvements in rice culture, animal husbandry, construction, education, medicine and science resulted. The religions of Buddhism and Taoism came, as well as Confucianism, which influenced the people's social lives. The foreign influx had the effect of creating in the people a desire for independence. Uprisings were not uncommon and these marked the start of thousands of years of fighting against foreign domination. The Trung sisters led the famous rebellion against the Chinese and, while it lasted for only three years (A.D. 40–43), they are remembered as the first heroines in their country's long struggle for independence. There are two pagodas dedicated to them in the northern part of the country and major streets in both Hanoi and Ho Chi Minh City are named "Hai Ba Trung" in memory of their early fight for Vietnam's independence. A longer-lasting rebellion was led by Ly Nam De when he thwarted the Chinese from A.D. 544 to 602. Direct Chinese domination lasted until 939 but was not truly removed until much later, in 1428.

The presence of such a powerful neighbour at its northern border has remained a strong influence in Vietnamese politics. Future subjugation and invasions have always been feared and the Vietnamese attitude towards the Chinese people who have remained in Vietnam reflects this.

South and Central Vietnam

Southern and central Vietnam escaped Chinese domination and were, instead, heavily influenced by the Indian civilisation introduced by sea traders and, indirectly, through the Khmer people. One of the most famous empires of the region was an early one, the Funan kingdom.

31

It covered most of the lower Mekong delta—including large portions of present-day south Vietnam, southern Cambodia and even parts of the Malay Peninsula—from the first to the sixth century A.D. Its influence extended into the interior where the Khmers lived and they integrated to form a strong coastal community dependent on maritime trade. The capital of Oc-Eo, near present-day Rach Gia, had an intricate system of canals winding through it that were thought to be used for irrigation as well as transportation. Various sea links have been traced by archaeologists who have uncovered an enormous variety of artifacts from the region. Gold Roman coins and Indonesian, Thai, Chinese, Indian and Greek objects have all been discovered. While this does not mean that there were direct links with these areas, it does indicate the power and wealth that the empire once had.

The southern region was the last part of modern-day Vietnam to be annexed by the Viets in the 18th century and to many Cambodians, it is still known as "Lower Cambodia". It became part of Vietnam in the late 1700s when the Tay Son Rebellion united most of present-day Vietnam. But a very strong Khmer influence is still felt in this region. Numerous Chams, Khmers and ethnic Chinese live within it although the Viets now make up by far the largest ethnic population. Instead of the Chinese-style Buddhist (Mahayana), Taoist and Confucianist mix of the north, the people were influenced by Hinduism and, later, a form of Buddhism known as Theravada. The foods are different, with more emphasis on spices and coconut milk, and the way of life is generally more relaxed.

Vietnam's borders have not been stable even in fairly recent times. The town of Ha Tien that lies along the Gulf of Thailand and near the Cambodian border was part of Cambodia until the early 1700s. When faced with increasing Thai attacks, the people turned from ineffective Cambodian protection and looked to Vietnam for help. More recently, there have been murderous incursions by the Khmer Rouge, and mines and booby traps still lie along the border.

Champa Kingdom

In the 2nd century A.D., the Champa kingdom started to emerge in central Vietnam, near Hue and Da Nang. It had the first written language of Southeast Asia and was a sophisticated, well-developed society, becoming very powerful and ruling until the mid-1600s. Now, it has been subsumed by the culture of the Viet people but the descendants of these Cham people are still clearly visible. They are of a different ethnic origin as they are of Austronesian stock, and are considered to be the pre-Chinese roots of the Vietnamese nation.

Ancient Cham towers are found all through the central coast and the ruins clearly show strong Hindu and Indian influences. At Nha Trang, the temple of Po Nagar was built from the 7th to the 12th centuries for Hindu worship. Today's Vietnamese Buddhists and Chinese recognise it as a holy site and still go there to make religious offerings. Just north of Qui Nhon are the remains of the Cham capital, Cha Ban, established around A.D. 1000. Despite harassment and plundering from the Khmers and Viets it held until the last great Cham battle against the Vietnamese. Emperor Le Thanh Ton overcame the Chams in 1471, taking over 60,000 Cham lives and imprisoning another 30,000. The city was subsequently used by the eldest of the three Tay Son brothers during the Tay Son Rebellion, but fell in 1801.

Cham culture was highly developed and its art shows a high level of refinement. Prior to the 10th century it was principally influenced by the Indonesians. The two had close contacts and scholars travelled regularly between Champa and Java. Later, Cham art reflected increasing Khmer and Viet influences but the overall projection is still Indian, with both Buddhist and Hindu effigies. Son My, north of Hoi An, is considered the finest Cham site in the country. When the Cham capital was situated at Simhapura (Tra Kieu) from the 4th to the 8th centuries, the intellectual and cultural centre was at Son My. It may also have been a burial site for the rulers. Experts believe it to have been on par with the great monuments which arose in other countries such as the Borobodur in Indonesia, Angkor Wat in Cambodia and

Pagan in Myanmar. It was known to be a religious centre as far back as the fourth century and was continually occupied until the 13th century. Since then, the buildings have suffered extensive pillaging and unfortunately high levels of bombing during the Vietnam War, but are now being restored. Da Nang has a Cham Museum containing the finest collection of these relics.

The Khmers to the west and south also influenced this long-lived kingdom and, depending on the strength of the rulers at the time, present-day southern Vietnam alternately came under Champa influence or was ruled by the Khmers.

The Rise and Fall of the Northern Vietnam Dynasties

With the downfall of the Tang dynasty in China at the end of the 10th century, the Vietnamese started to exert their independence and several short-lived dynasties came and went. Each ruled independently of the Chinese but recognised itself as a vassal state and sent a triennial tribute. The Ly dynasty, which lasted from 1010 to 1225, fought and gained true independence and also pushed the Champa kingdom in central Vietnam further south. During this reign, Buddhism flourished and monks held high political positions and acted as the king's advisers. But the last of the Ly kings had no male heir and political turmoil followed his death, resulting in the emergence of the Tran dynasty, best known for its successful struggle against the Mongol conqueror, Kublai Khan. It was troubled with internal problems, being harassed from the south by the Champa and from the north by the Chinese. The Chinese called northern Vietnam "Annam", meaning "The Pacified South", and it again became a vassal state to the Ming dynasty of China and was under its direct control from 1406 to 1427.

Still regarded as a hero in present-day Vietnam, Le Loi helped create the golden age of Vietnamese dynasties, the Later Le dynasty (1427–1789). During this reign, the Champa Kingdom in the south was virtually wiped out while, internally, the administrative system was reformed. Traditional Vietnamese culture flourished, replacing Chinese ideas. For instance, traditional Vietnamese law was used once again instead of the Chinese legal system. Vietnamese literature became popular, although Confucianism was still dominant in the upper stratas of society. Later in the period, the Trinh and Nguyen families from the north and south, respectively, became very strong and ruled through the weaker Le Loi monarchs. In the south, the Mekong delta area, up to the Gulf of Thailand, was annexed from the Khmers and in the early 1800s, parts of Cambodia and Laos had to accept Vietnamese sovereignty for a short period.

Foreign Influences

The Later Le dynasty was the first to be exposed to the Catholic missionaries who arrived with Western traders. In the early 1500s, the Portuguese came from their colony of Macau and, over time, the Chinese, Japanese, Dutch and French also came to trade. The rulers feared these foreigners, particularly the Catholics and Jesuits, believing that they brought subversive Western ideas that challenged Confucianism. This fear proved to be well-founded. The Dutch supported the northern Trinh family and the French, the Nguyens. Each provided military assistance for the feuding between the two until a truce was reached eventually and the country was divided between them along the River Gianh.

Continual warring between the families left the country in administrative chaos. The Tay Son Rebellion (1771–1802) thus erupted, supported by peasants who were fed up with corrupt overlords, and Nguyen Hue, its leader, took control of central Vietnam. By 1783, the Nguyen family was ousted and Saigon was controlled by the rebels. Soon afterwards, the Trinhs were defeated and all of Vietnam was united. Nguyen Anh, the only prince from the southern family to survive the attack, fought back with French help and in 1802, under the name of Gia Long, took control of all of Vietnam. He established Hue as his capital, gave the French considerable commercial concessions for their help and started a major infrastructure programme for the country. Administrative reforms were implemented, land was redistributed, uniform weights and measures were introduced, coins were minted and the national language was used where possible.

However, Nguyen Anh's son and his future successors were strongly Confucian and slowly, the benefits given to the French were removed. At the same time, there was a backlash against the Catholic missionaries who had been working hard to gain Vietnamese converts. The pro-Chinese successors ordered the persecution of the Catholics and in doing so, gave the French an excuse to intervene in the country. The French government occupied the port of Tourane (present-day Da Nang) in August 1858 and by 1861, had taken Saigon. The Vietnamese emperors, following an isolationist policy, crumbled as the French went on to occupy all of southern Vietnam and christen it as the French colony of Cochin-China. Central Vietnam was annexed, renamed Annam and allowed to keep a puppet emperor while northern Vietnam, renamed Tonkin, became a colony ruled by the French.

Just as Chinese domination had introduced new ideas, concepts and technology, so did the French presence. New architectural styles were introduced and foods and agricultural patterns evolved as rubber, coffee and tea plantations were established. Saigon became known as the "Paris of the Orient" and education, medical care and administrative reforms were introduced.

The Independence Movement

Naturally, the Vietnamese resented French dominance as much as they had the Chinese. Numerous factions aiming for reform, democracy and independence rose and fell but the French remained in command. The Russian revolution inspired Nguyen That Thanh, better known under his later alias of Ho Chi Minh. After working with Phan Chu Trinh on an anti-colonial petition for the Versailles Conference of 1919, he became involved with a French group that went on to form the French Communist Party. He received support from the communists and travelled to Russia, becoming enamoured with their ideas. Later, he went on to China where he founded the Association of Vietnamese Youth. In 1930, Ho Chi Minh founded the Indo-Chinese Communist Party and small uprisings modelled on the Chinese Kuomintang revolt were staged, but were quashed by the French.

World War II then shattered the region's politics and the Japanese invaded Vietnam as they advanced southwards in 1940. The French Vichy government accepted the occupation of Indo-China and, as compensation, were allowed to continue governing the colony, only to be ousted by the Japanese in March 1945 when the Allied victory in Europe was becoming a certainty. As Japan fell later the same year, a political vacuum resulted and Ho Chi Minh, with the backing of the Viet Minh, a group formed by the Indo-Chinese Communist Party for revolutionary purposes, promptly began taking control of as much territory as possible before the Allies arrived.

On September 2, 1945, Ho Chi Minh proclaimed himself president of the Democratic Republic of Vietnam. Despite some progress at the negotiating table, the Vietnamese found themselves heading into a decade-long guerrilla war for independence against the French. This began at the end of 1946. However, there were divisions within the independence movement when the communist nature of Ho Chi Minh's revolutionary group began to emerge. The United States had become increasingly concerned about the worldwide spread of communism and its "domino effect" through Asia. So they supported the French against Ho Chi Minh's revolutionary forces by providing massive amounts of aid. Despite this, the ground-swell of support from the Vietnamese was too strong. Their determination to win became obvious with their colossal defeat of the French Expeditionary Forces at the "impregnable" fortress of Dien Bien Phu. Official independence came soon afterwards on July 20, 1954, after long discussions in Geneva. The country was split at the 17th parallel pending general elections on reunification scheduled for the middle of 1956. The north became the Democratic Republic of Vietnam under the Vietnamese Workers Party (a group set up by Ho Chi Minh, also known as Lao Dong) and the south became the Republic of South Vietnam.

Peace never came and the elections were not held. Instead, civil war between the two republics erupted. Ngo Dinh Diem, leader of the South, gained formal recognition internationally as he was Catholic and anti-communist. Because of religious intolerance, most of the Catholics from the north fled south in 1954, resettling on the outskirts of Saigon, where today a proliferation of churches can be seen marking their new home.

Ho Chi Minh's Northern regime started its bid to reunify Vietnam in 1959. The Ho Chi Minh trail was begun and it quickly became an invaluable link to filter men and equipment southwards and a communication line northwards, keeping the Northern leaders in touch with the progress. By the early 1960s the Viet Cong, a Southern communist movement, had emerged and was rapidly gaining local support, with many Viet Minhs joining the ranks. Soon, it attracted the support of infiltrators from communist North Vietnam as well. Repression of the Buddhists and a series of destabilising *coup d'etats* resulted in a weakening of the South Vietnamese government. As the communist insurgency gained strength, the Americans realised that a substantial increase in direct involvement would be required to prop up the South Vietnamese government.

For peasants, the war was not necessarily about communism versus democracy, but about the poor versus the rich, Buddhists against Catholics, rural dwellers against city people and independence versus foreign domination. Also, while Westerners find it hard to understand how the masses accepted communism, it must be remembered that prior to European domination, the Vietnamese had been accustomed to a high level of interference in all aspects of daily life. Emperors were feudal and at times very dictatorial, and so the

Changing of the guard at the Ho Chi Minh Mausoleum in Hanoi.

movement towards a strong bureaucracy that controlled so many aspects of daily life was not that difficult. On top of this. the structure of Vietnamese politics is not as centrally controlled as. for instance, that of the former USSR or China. Each local area still exerted considerable autonomy.

The Vietnam War

John F. Kennedy was elected president of the United States in 1961 and through the fear of the "domino effect"—which would have caused countries in Southeast Asia to fall to the communists one by one—he brought the containment of communism to the forefront of U.S. foreign policy. In 1965. the United States dramatically raised the number of men and the amount of equipment involved and sent in the first official combat troops, rather than just the military advisers they had previously claimed to be using.

In 1964, the war had spread from South Vietnam to include the North as well. Over a 10-year period, more than 10 million military personnel were sent to the country. Most were American but Koreans, Thais, Australians, New Zealanders and non-combat support staff from over 30 other countries were included too.

By the mid-1960s, however, support for the war by the American people was falling dramatically and the economic strain was being felt. In 1968, the long-drawn peace negotiations started. Ho Chi Minh, the North's venerated leader, died the following year. 1969 also saw the start of U.S. bombing raids into Cambodia in an effort to break the north-south trail and the beginning of a gradual U.S. military withdrawal. The withdrawal accelerated after the 1973 Paris Peace Agreements, leaving only a few advisers in South Vietnam. The North seized the opportunity and broke its ceasefire agreement, with Viet Cong tanks breaking through the gates of the presidential palace in Saigon on April 30, 1975. It was an image seen by millions on television screens across the world and marked the success of the communists in finally uniting Vietnam under their banner.

The next year, nationwide elections were held and the country formally took on the name of the Socialist Republic of Vietnam. The current government structure is outlined in the Resources chapter at the end of this book.

A Short Peace

Despite unification, economic progress was not forthcoming. The country struggled to consolidate itself and the re-education process to socialism began for the south. Many refugees fled the country as "boat people" seeking a better life elsewhere. By the end of 1978, Vietnamese troops were again fighting, this time in neighbouring Cambodia, as they sought to oust Pol Pot's genocidal regime and his Khmer Rouge forces. They achieved this goal but became embroiled in regional politics again when the Chinese invaded their northern borders in 1979. The Chinese were supporting the Khmer Rouge forces and sought to teach Vietnam a lesson for meddling in Cambodia's politics. With China's encouragement, Vietnam became ostracised internationally for its role in the Cambodian war. Led by the United States, an economic embargo was placed on the country.

The joint impact of the trade embargo and the draining effect of deploying troops in Cambodia further weakened Vietnam economically. Enormous technological and economic support had been provided by the USSR but this dried up as the Soviet Union dissolved. Vietnam realised it had to make dramatic changes to restructure its economy. By September 1989, all troops in Cambodia had been withdrawn as part of the "road-map to normalisation" that had been developed in conjunction with the international community. As *glasnost* and *perestroika* altered the course of the USSR's economy, Vietnam realised it needed to follow suit.

After the Sixth Party Congress in December 1986, wide-ranging economic reforms, known collectively as *Doi Moi* (Renovation), were introduced, making foreign investment and the stimulation of the economy national priorities. Most Western nations have now normalised relations with Vietnam. Wary of the rapidly destabilising changes that have occurred in the former USSR, the Vietnamese government has continued on a cautious path of improving free market trade while maintaining its communist objectives.

History Lessons

But while the Vietnam War changed the psyche of Americans and many others—and political analysts see it as a turning point in the way the United States dealt with foreign affairs—to the Vietnamese, it was just one more war in a long history of wars. They have spent thousands of years struggling for freedom and peace and are finally being rewarded. The Vietnamese take great pride in knowing that they have defeated the Chinese, French, Japanese and, finally, the United States and its allies. They are proud of their resilience and show more confidence in their own abilities than many other Asian races. In older people, this may manifest itself quietly; despite short-term setbacks, they do not give up their goal or long-term commitment towards achieving a task. Younger people, however, voice it more openly and throw out challenges.

The Vietnamese firmly believe they are the best. The Chinese summarise this in a saying: "Vietnam is nobody's lapdog." They will not be the lapdog of foreign business powers either.

VIETNAM TODAY

The Economy

Vietnam is undergoing rapid change. As the politics alter and the communist government relaxes its foreign investment policies, money and technology have started to flow into the country and it is starting to prosper again. The economy still revolves largely around agriculture and oil products. Major exports are rice, timber, coal, coffee, rubber and crude oil, while the principal imports consist of oil products and fertilisers. But the economy is diversifying. Overseas investment has brought with it new ideas, up-to-date technology and managerial techniques that are all having positive effects.

Continual warring has drained the country's wealth and taken a heavy toll on its people but peace is now being enjoyed and Vietnam is springing back to its feet. The impetus is coming from several sources. Internally, the government is freeing the economy from controls and has reigned in inflation. The Gross Domestic Product is steadily growing and the *dong,* the Vietnamese unit of currency, remains relatively stable. There is still much work to be done and the current overhaul of the country's infrastructure, investment laws and banking procedures will help the continued improvements.

Problems

The state of transition that the country is now in is not all smooth and rosy. There has been a rapid movement of people from the country to the cities, particularly Ho Chi Minh City. Most are hoping to make their fortune, and the mass movement of people places great strains on the infrastructure of the city. The roads were once relatively quiet and the bicycle was the main form of transport, but motorcycles and cars are now rapidly clogging roads not designed for their use or numbers. With this has come a dramatic increase in road accidents.

Things that were free until recently—such as primary school education—must now be paid for. Unemployment is quite high. The official estimate in 1993 was 18–19% but unofficially, the figure was thought to be much higher.

On a personal basis, the lack of contact with foreigners in Vietnam's recent history is reflected both in charming naïveté and frustrating misunderstandings. The absence of background knowledge of Western-style business habits requires more detailed training programmes than would otherwise be necessary.

Rules, Regulations and Crackdowns

The situation here is still far from settled and rules seem to change on an almost daily basis. The Vietnamese are very pragmatic. They acknowledge the need for overseas money and know-how. But the government fluctuates in its attitude towards foreign culture and the presence of foreign residents. Increasingly, the government sees overseas visitors as a source of income for the country and new taxes and charges are increasing steadily. The changes can make it very hard for foreign businesses to estimate the costs and profits of future projects.

The extent to which foreigners are free to conduct their business is also in a state of flux. While the government welcomes foreign business acumen, they do not always appreciate the foreign ways that are introduced and police intervention can and does occur. There are also periodic "tightening up" activities, often just prior to National Day or Labour Day.

The Impact on the People

The physical and mental toll exacted by the Vietnam War, together with the hard years that followed, are still visible. The demographics have been skewed with many young men lost in the fighting. Amputees and people with mental problems, together with continuing birth defects from chemicals used, place strains on the hospitals and support networks. Many earn a living as beggars. In a casual taxi ride, post-1975 hardship stories are common. There is resentment at the way jobs and access to education have subsequently been handed out.

Warfare has changed the way the Vietnamese think and approach life. In the past, it was possible to execute ideas quickly before political changes or the tragedies of war upset the planning process. Short-term goals took priority then but now, with economic and political stability, people are returning to a more balanced view.

To get to know the Vietnamese well can be a frustrating road, and not just because of the language barrier. Until you become firm friends, you may only know superficial details about your contacts' family and background. Traditionally, the people are shy and re-served. The problems of the Vietnam War, subsequent "re-education" by the communists and the close observation of anyone suspected of helping the South Vietnamese regime have made many wary of friendships with foreigners; they prefer not to talk of wealth, family or future plans. This is slowly changing but they remain reticent.

History has given them a very strong self-preservation instinct which includes rage, revenge and grudges held against those seen to be getting in their way. At the lower levels of society, such matters may be resolved by stealing, using black magic to make someone ill or delivering self-styled justice with a knife. Foreigners are not exempt from such actions so it would be wise not to offend anyone.

Changing Generations

Recent history has produced a country with a very distinct generation gap among the people. The experiences and political systems that the different generations have lived through over the past few decades have strongly shaped their views on life. The differences between the young and old are more obvious in the north, where the change from a very closed political system to a more open one has been greater than in the south.

Many of the traditional values of the Vietnamese have recently become diluted. In the recent past, a woman would not sit next to a man unless he was her husband. Now, a young woman will ride pillion on a motorcycle with her arms around the male rider and young couples can be seen holding hands and kissing in parks during the evenings. The government is showing concern over the changes in standards and values. Until 1975, Vietnamese traditions, values and social customs were taught in school. They were subsequently dropped from the curriculum but reintroduced in 1984 when the consequences of their removal became apparent.

In his book, *A Dragon Apparent,* Norman Lewis tells the story of a bus hitting a cyclist during French colonial times. The cyclist was unhurt but his bicycle was badly mangled. The bus driver jumped out and raced to congratulate the cyclist, who was beaming. Both thanked their good fortune that the cyclist was unhurt. Today, if the same situation were to occur, both would still consider themselves lucky but any amenability would probably be replaced by an argument over the cost of repairing the bicycle.

Beauty has always been in the eye of the beholder. Upper-class Vietnamese girls, as they reached puberty, used to have their teeth blackened permanently with a lacquer. Now, only older women are seen with such teeth. Young city girls would rather spend a great deal of time attending to their personal hygiene and Western-style make-up. Long, black hair is giving way to Western perms and colouring.

The Older Generation

The older people are very polite, tolerant, patient and, not surprisingly, have a world-weary way about them. Their lives have seen dramatic changes from French colonial times and the days of the mandarins to American intervention, years of warfare and hardship and, finally, independence. These changes were accompanied by economic hardship in the early days but there is now growing peace and prosperity.

For the people, family and village community ties remain strong. They have always lived as an extended family group and many would not have survived without such close associations. French is still widely spoken among the better educated and, for a long time, was the principal language used at university level.

The Middle-Aged

While middle-aged Vietnamese may be influenced by Western culture, they usually continue to respect traditional ways. They tend to prefer to live with their immediate family group. The better-educated speak Russian as many studied in universities in the USSR or were sent there for training.

Young Vietnamese

The young are generally materialistic and keen to learn. Television and videos keep them up to date with news and sports and have introduced them to a Western lifestyle. For the younger set, close family ties are losing their importance. Some would like to live by themselves for a few years but few can afford it. Many have to move to find a job and they feel great pressure to achieve and get ahead in life. The suicide rate among this group is quite high although official statistics are unavailable. The traditional concept of a strong nation wielding its influence on strong family ties is disappearing rapidly. For the young, English is the most important language as it has become the language of business in Vietnam.

Such differences between the generations, however, are not based on age alone. In the country, people still live an agrarian life, tend to be more traditional and hold a stronger set of beliefs than those residing in the cities. Farmers and fishermen enjoy a slower lifestyle and many attribute occurrences to fate. City dwellers, on the other hand, find themselves caught up in a faster pace of life, see direct results from their actions and experience the frustrations and pressure often associated with urban life.

The People of the Regions

There are regional differences that are also a product of history, as well as geography. Physically, the country is spread over a long stretch of land and the people differ racially from region to region. Their roots vary as the ancient north was more exposed to Chinese ways while the south had greater influence from the Khmers and Chams. Each region has its own religious beliefs and, in more recent history, the north has been through a longer period of austerity and has experienced a more fervent form of communism than the south. Furthermore, as the climate changes along Vietnam's length, so does the ecology and the means by which the people support themselves.

During recent times, however, the differences have been downplayed. The subject is regarded as politically sensitive as the government is trying to project the country as a unified whole. Elsewhere in the world, people joke about political, geographical and cultural differences within a country. Vietnam is no exception, in spite of the sensitivities involved. There are innuendos in jokes that speculate on what a northerner or southerner would do upon winning a lottery, for instance. It is said that the northerner would re-roof his house while a southerner would buy a television set.

The people from the north are thought to have the tendency of avoiding decision-making. This may be because of their traditional ways and their preference for consensus in order to maintain social harmony. Such indecision tends to be a feature of large bureaucracies—and a communist government—as the people are unsure of where the decision-making power actually lies. Or it may be because they are afraid to take the responsibility that comes with making a decision. Historians also point out that the northerners have worked public or imperial land for centuries. Decisions concerning what crops to grow and when to grow them were made by appointed officials. In the south, where land was mostly owned privately, people from all walks of life had to develop decision-making skills. This, together with the more recent foreign influence, has led to different business techniques developing between the two areas.

There is a much stronger feeling of working together for a common goal in the north compared with the south. Whether this is because, historically, the people have worked common ground or because the communist work ethic is stronger is impossible to say. The sense of competition, particularly for commercial gain, is much stronger in the south.

The irony lies in the fact that southerners who have an abundance of food are often regarded by northerners as lazy. Things grow easily and famines and disease are infrequent. Southerners maintain they work as hard as those in the north, but admit that they are certainly more ready to spend their money. They do not plan for the future, are more ostentatious in their ways, and more direct in discussions. Their greater exposure to foreign influence makes them open to new ideas and they appear more dynamic in action and modern in appearance.

Central and northern Vietnamese are perceived as being more hardworking, patient and prudent than their southern counterparts. They plan for the future as food supply is less readily available and the weather is not as predictable. Northerners are more far-sighted, think through different options and do not reveal their feelings easily. Others see them either of two ways: as ambitious and crafty, or tactful, discreet and diplomatic. A southerner would look for ulterior motives in an invitation from a northerner. Offsetting this view, some would rather do business with northerners, who are characterised as being more straightforward in their ways, than with southerners, whose conversation may be direct but whose entrepreneurial spirit may result in less than fair dealings with others.

Parts of the central region are very poor and conditions there have helped breed wiry, dauntless people such as Ho Chi Minh, the scholar Nguyen Cong Tru and poet Nguyen Du. Central people had to be clever and cunning to survive and people feel they have to tread very carefully when dealing with them. Qualifications are held in high regard and other status indicators are also very important to them, perhaps because Hue, in the central region, was the imperial court and educational centre for so long.

In the different geographical regions of Vietnam, spurious statements are often made about each other—for instance, those from the central area are regarded as having low morals, and there are stories of wives being offered to bosses for business favours! Many of these comments are made in a light-hearted manner but underneath the banter, people from one region view those from another with suspicion. They make gross generalities about each other that are widely held.

People usually marry and employ staff from the same region as themselves. Instances of staff discriminating against a new employee from a different region are not uncommon. This is aggravated by the fact that in the past 40 years or so, people have been very mobile and there are many northerners living in the south and vice versa.

Migration Waves

Traditionally, people have strong emotional links with their land, not just because it provides them with food, but also because ancestral burial plots have to be cared for. In recent years, warfare, politics and urbanisation have dragged people from their roots. Many have travelled south, sometimes in waves. Two distinct migration periods were 1954 and post-1975. The first period saw people leaving north Vietnam when the French fell. Many were Catholics. The second major move came after South Vietnam was "liberated". People of the correct political persuasion were required to fill specific jobs and so many northerners moved south. Southerners still refer to someone as a north-'54 or north-'75 person, categorising them according to the migration period.

But while the differences are there, the people are still Vietnamese. They are proud of their country and achievements. They want to catch up with their Southeast Asian neighbours in business terms but not at the expense of their culture or way of life. They will simply look for methods of achieving success the Vietnamese way. The people have a saying that a man can eat Chinese food, live in a French house and marry a Japanese wife, but he is still Vietnamese. In other words, the Vietnamese are able to adapt foreign ideas to suit their own purposes.

Chapter Three

THE PEOPLE

When foreigners talk about Vietnam, memories of the Vietnam War, the boat people fleeing the country and trade embargoes often come to mind. From 1975 until the mid-1980s, the country was cut off from most of the outside world. Hence, visitors remember the political issues and first impressions of the country are often qualified in these terms. They are surprised that there is little open resentment towards foreigners and specifically, towards those from the United States, despite the enormous suffering inflicted on all Vietnamese during the Vietnam War. Most foreigners know little about the people or their daily life and understanding these, together with the country's history, will help them realise why their first impression is rarely upheld.

The Vietnamese

As with any other nationality, to provide a brief description of the Vietnamese is to talk in gross generalities about a diverse mixture of people. Fifty-four different ethnic groups are recognised here. Add to these the ethnic Chinese who have lived here for generations, the French who have settled as well as the other nationalities of expatriates and everyday life becomes a minefield of cultural nuances. Amerasians can be added to the mixing pot, creating another face shape and set of issues. But the Viets are the dominant racial group and comprise about 84% of the population. So, naturally, their culture and language prevail and it is these that will be discussed here primarily.

The people are pragmatic and have a burning desire to catch up with their neighbours in terms of economic wealth. They display great courtesy, maintain strong family bonds and revere the old and those in authority (thanks to Confucianist principles). So they may appear modest, humble and reserved. The need to preserve social harmony makes them prefer consensus to decision-making in all walks of life. Women hold jobs and are confident partners in society.

ETHNIC GROUPS

The Viets (or Kinh) have a Sino (Chinese) origin. The remaining ethnicities are usually grouped either by language or racial derivation. They are fascinatingly diverse and it is beyond the scope of this book to deal with each in detail but it is well worth reading some of the background literature on them (see the further reading suggestions in the Bibliography). Many live in the highlands and are related to Thailand's hill tribes. Groups have interbred and clear distinctions are no longer always possible. Historical upheavals have resulted in migrations of small groups or large-scale movements. The language, ethnographics, demography and cultural aspects of both the new settlers and existing residents have altered with every move. As a result, ethnicity is often blurred and can occur in geographically divergent regions.

Viets

Today's Viet ethnic group evolved in the north of the country between the 2nd century B.C. and 2nd century A.D. Their original racial stock was a mixture of Indonesian, Chinese, immigrant Thai and earlier Viet stock from further north. Subsequently, they have been strongly influenced by the Chinese and indirectly by the Indians through the Champa and Khmer kingdoms. As they were principally rice growers, they have preferred the lowlands and spread south along the coast.

Ethno-linguistic Minorities

Vietnam has a very complicated mix of minority groups. Populations vary from no more than a few hundred to over 1.5 million. The French called them *montagnards*, meaning highlanders, and the Viets often referred to them as the *moi*, meaning savages, as they felt that the hill people were not as culturally refined as themselves. The minority groups have had little access to formal education and their role in the economy is negligible. Most Vietnamese do not hold them in high regard and they are now termed "national minorities".

The minorities can be classified into three main categories according to language: the Austro-Asian family includes the Bru, Cua, Hre, Rengao, Sedang, Bahnar, Muong, Tay, Mnong, Ma, Stieng and Thai; the Malayo-Polynesian family include the Jarai, Rhade, Raglai and Chu Ru; and the Sino-Tibetans include the Hoa, Lolo and Ha Nhi. The languages within one family may be quite unintelligible to another within the same family and the diversity in regard to culture and social customs is vast.

In the past, when most were semi-nomadic carrying out agriculture using slash-and-burn principles, an area would remain fallow for 10 to 20 years. Now, the migration of lowland people into the hills, and the hill tribes' increasing population, mean that good agricultural land in the highlands is in short supply. Areas are not left fallow for long enough and the people are not able to support themselves in the traditional manner. They are being encouraged by the Vietnamese government to shift to sedentary farming practices which would allow better access to health care and education. It would make the adjustment into the social and political mainstream of Vietnamese life easier. But there is a strong distrust of the lowland people, who have historically pushed them from better land further into the hilltops, and so there is resistance.

Hill tribe woman smoking a pipe.

In the past, most hill tribes were off-limits to foreign visitors but now, with permits, it is possible to meet some of them. Each tribe has its own characteristics and the extent to which the various tribes are being assimilated into the Vietnamese way of life and giving up their traditional dress differs. If you travel in the hills, it is advisable to read up on the specific groups you are likely to meet. For instance, the Lat people near Da Lat are matriarchal and live in longhouses. When a daughter marries, her husband joins her and an extension is made to the longhouse of the bride's family to accommodate the new couple. Each couple have their own entrance, so the number of stairs indicates the number of families living in any one longhouse. But only a few of the Lat people still live this way and most live in single family houses.

Chams

There are an estimated 60,000–100,000 Chams in the country who are descendants of a once-flourishing Champa Kingdom in central Vietnam. It existed from the 2nd to 15th centuries before being overrun by the southward-moving Viets. Most of the latter-day Chams still live in the central zone. Some still wear traditional clothes and adhere to their customs and religion but many are quite well assimilated and are not easily recognisable. Now, the Chams of Thuan Hai who fled south in the 1600s have converted to Islam but those in An Guang province have remained Hindu. Buddhism was also important in the past. The people's language falls into the Malayo-Polynesian group. Interestingly, they are matriarchal in nature, with the women controlling all family and religious matters.

The Cham Kingdom is still famous as many of its towering temples can be seen scattered throughout the country. The brick constructions reflect the strong Indian influence.

Khmers

The Khmers are of Cambodian descent and the vast majority of the estimated 700,000 in Vietnam live in the Mekong delta as this region was ruled by Khmer kingdoms for thousands of years. Others are more recent escapees from the Pol Pot regime in Cambodia. Irrigated rice cultivation, fruit and vegetable farming, fishing and weaving are the principal activities. The people are mostly Buddhist, but of the Theravada sect. Both Brahmanism and the Indian culture have influenced the Khmers and elements of this are still clearly visible. Their language type is Austro-Asian. The social organisation is patrilineal but women have considerable influence within the household and in divorce and inheritance matters.

Ethnic Chinese

The Chinese influence permeated all aspects of Vietnamese life and they still have a great deal of influence over the local economy. With over 10 centuries of Chinese domination in the country's history and the close proximity of the two countries, it is not surprising that many ethnic Chinese still live in Vietnam. Some have integrated well, intermarrying with the Viets, while others have remained as distinct groups. They socialise within their own *bangs,* or associations based on the area of China from which they originated. This also determines the dialect spoken. Cholon, a district of Ho Chi Minh City, is home to the greatest concentration of ethnic Chinese. At different times in the country's history, there have been active political moves to assimilate, segregate or even oust the Chinese.

Most Chinese tend to be very superstitious. Their religion is a mixture of ancestor worship, Taoism, Buddhism, animism, Confucianism and, for some, Christianity or Islam as well. The family unit is very powerful and patrilineal. Women play a subservient role, being barred from many activities. They are usually expected to stay at home and look after the family.

Known throughout the world for their business acumen, the people play an important role in the local economy, concentrating on financial and mechanical areas. They are considered to be shrewd business partners who choose to emphasise long-term relationships.

Viet Kieu

Unlike each of the previous groups, this term does not describe a racial division, but refers to Vietnamese who have left their homeland and become citizens of another country. Most are originally from South Vietnam. During the last 50 years, large numbers of people have left and settled in the United States, Canada, France and Australia, many under the recent Orderly Departure Scheme. Some left for political reasons, others for economic or educational reasons. Like all Vietnamese, they maintain strong ties with their extended family members who are still living in Vietnam. Over Tet, the traditional time for gift-giving, millions of dollars enter Vietnam in the form of money or gifts for family and friends, giving the economy a boost.

Many Viet Kieu are also returning to Vietnam to set up businesses. They understand the cultural differences and have the family contacts to be successful, while being able to provide the set-up capital and technical knowledge. Although some of the Vietnamese do not trust them, the government is increasingly wooing this set of people in an effort to reconstruct the country's economy.

Boat People

Unlike the Viet Kieu who left successfully and started a new life in another country, others have tried to leave, but were not accepted for residence by another country. Whether they left by land or boat, this group are collectively known as boat people. (Although many of the Viet Kieu were also boat people, they managed to gain residence in another country.) Nobody knows how many boat people there are or were, but the estimate is well over 100,000. Some did not survive the perils of starvation and piracy in their efforts to leave and many others were caught and are still being detained in camps abroad. Others tried to return but were turned back by the Vietnamese authorities and some remain illegal immigrants in other countries.

Camps were set up in neighbouring countries to deal with the exodus in the late 1980s. In 1991, the number of people in such camps peaked at 120,000. By 1994, it was estimated that about 54,000 refugees still remained. These people are now considered economic rather than political refugees. A voluntary repatriation scheme has been in operation for some time and it is hoped that all will be assimilated back into Vietnam.

THEIR WAY OF LIFE

Community

A strong sense of community is felt by all Vietnamese, including those who live in large cities. It is an intrinsic part of their make-up and ethnographers believe it stems from their long reliance on wet rice agriculture. Rice was first domesticated in the Yangtze delta in China 7,000 years ago and had spread to the Red River delta in North Vietnam by 2,500–2,000 B.C., according to archaeologists. The people had to cooperate and work together on intra-village irrigation systems to get the benefits of a good harvest. This created a sense of unity between villages as the mono-culture spread from area to area.

Village life is simple and revolves around the seasons. Many rural areas still do not have electricity. On the periphery of the northern villages, large bamboos are often planted to serve as a fence and to provide shade, as well as a ready supply of building material. The village centre is marked by the *dinh,* a combined temple and community centre. Houses are constructed of local timber, straw and bamboo or, more frequently, clay bricks made nearby. Toilets are located away from the house and, maybe, sited over a pond. Each family usually has livestock, a fish pond and a small vegetable plot.

Families

As in many parts of Asia, life revolves around the family. People live in extended families that usually include three generations comprising grandparents, parents and children. Children obey their parents and a 20-year-old girl may be forbidden to go out after 6 p.m. This may be a throwback to a time when the city was not a safe place at night. Older members of the family or community are seen as wise and their views are greatly respected. The fast changes in Vietnam's economy have seen this respect eroded a little and one of the few areas where younger members of the family contradict their elders is with regard to today's market forces.

Close contact is always maintained between family members. Geographical separations are bridged by regular telephone calls. Owing to the strong link with their ancestors, the people are also attached to family land where their dead are buried. Financially, they will help each other, giving money or buying presents that meet the needs of family members. It is more of an obligation than a voluntary gesture of generosity. This family strength has helped the people survive their turbulent history. Together with the sense of community and family belonging goes an emphasis on maintaining social harmony. Its extent can be seen in Chapter 6, Communication and Chapter 7, Socialising in Vietnam. Consensus is always preferred and individual decision-making is avoided

Marriage and Morality

Everyone is expected to marry, although with the skewing of the population statistics due to war, many women have been unable to find a partner.

It is very important that women are virgins on their wedding night, so young girls are carefully chaperoned during their courting days. The influence of the Vietnam War and the current crop of rebellious youngsters who subscribe to foreign ways of thinking are exceptions to this. Men, however, are more promiscuous and many visit prostitutes before and even after marriage. The wife, however, is expected to remain faithful to her husband.

Having a child out of wedlock is not socially acceptable, with mothers suffering family rejection and often finding it impossible to get a job. Since 1993, it has become legally possible not to state the name of the father on a child's birth certificate. Divorce is now accepted and can be initiated by the husband or wife.

Children

It is considered a tragedy not to marry and have children. Children are the most important feature in a marriage. Because of this, an expectant mother does not travel after the first month of pregnancy so as to avoid mishaps, but the traditional periods of confinement both before and after birth are now less strictly observed.

Large families of 10–15 used to be common, although the mortality rate was quite high. Children were regarded as a sort of pension in one's old age. The more children a couple had, the luckier they were seen to be. Now, the costs of raising and educating children and the government drive to reduce population growth has affected the birth rate, and many city parents choose to have only two children. Sons are preferred as they will continue the family line and make offerings to their parents' souls after death. Girls, on the other hand, get married and leave their own family to join their husbands. Birth control has not been readily available or affordable. Traditionally, the father and sons sleep in the front of the house with the ancestral shrine and the daughters and mother sleep in the back (considered the lower) part of the house. This arrangement in itself helps to control the birth rate! Condoms are increasingly available but many women have turned to abortions, which sometimes result in health problems.

All children are expected to work hard. From a young age, they will help with chores around the house. Boys and girls cook, clean and care for their younger siblings while their mother is at work, although such housework is done mainly by the girls. The eldest son is responsible for the moral upbringing of his siblings, such as ensuring that they do their homework. He is also ultimately responsible for the finances of the whole family, caring for the parents when they are old and paying homage to the ancestors, although all the children will contribute money to their parents to help support them later in life.

Education

Education has traditionally been held in very high regard. Vietnam's first national university was founded in 1076, two centuries before Britain's Oxford University. Considering the country's economic standards, it has an exceptionally high literacy level of 82%. Almost all children go to primary school and 30–40% attend secondary school. There are numerous universities and colleges and many parents and children strive to gain access to these. The emphasis comes not only from a desire to get a better job, but also from Confucian beliefs that a person's level of education reflects his status and identity.

However, educational attainment has been decreasing in recent years. Up till 1989, the first 12 years of education were free but this has been cut down to the first three years. While the costs are still very low, economic pressures are encouraging parents to put their children into jobs from an early age. Teachers used to hold a highly respected position in the community but their salaries have been eroded under the new political order and theirs is now a poorly paid job. Many have to teach private classes after school in order to survive. University entrance requirements for teachers are now lower than for most other professions.

School classes usually run from 7 a.m. to 11.15 a.m., and from 1 p.m. to 5 p.m. Because there is a shortage of teachers and school space, many children only attend one of these two sessions. Vietnamese schools have a long, three-month break over summer, running approximately from the beginning of June until early September. They take another two weeks off over the Tet, or New Year, season.

Working Life

The day starts at dawn for most people and, even in the city, most people are up and about by 5.30 a.m. Many people can be seen going through their *tai chi* exercises in a park or open area. Visits to the market are conducted early and on a daily basis as there is much

61

emphasis on fresh ingredients and many homes do not have refrigerators. After this, people go off to work or school.

Work usually starts at 7–7.30 a.m. Everyone stops for lunch around 11–11.30 a.m. and families go home to eat together, then relax and enjoy a siesta through the heat of the day. Work commences around 1.30–2 p.m. and finishes at 4–4.30 p.m. Many people stop early to take on a second job and earn more money. They return home by about 6.30 p.m. for dinner, which is a family affair. By 10–11 p.m. most people would have gone to sleep.

Sexual Equality

The mother is the principal caregiver of the family. She shops and does most of the household chores. She may get some assistance from grandparents, younger sisters or older daughters who help care for the children as she works. Childcare facilities are also available. Men tend to have more leisure time and fathers spend a good deal of it helping the children with their homework or playing with them.

Vietnamese women are used to working. Vietnam has rarely had long periods of peace and through the deprivations of war, women had to run the household besides working in the fields and taking on additional work to support the family. This equality has been strengthened under communism and it is not unusual to see women in positions of power within the government. The Women's Union was started in 1930 and wields considerable influence.

Legally, men and women have equality in most areas. The 1959 Marriage and Family Law Act states that sons and daughters must be treated equally while the 1986 Act says that childcare and household duties are the equal responsibility of husband and wife. In practice, women do the bulk of household chores and mind the children while working outside the home as well. Most are employed in poorer paying jobs which involve manual labour, such as in rice agriculture or animal husbandry. Many are employed on a seasonal basis. The Western feminist movement is not seen as an appropriate model here.

Class Structure

In the past, a strong class structure existed with the mandarins at the top, a middle class of city people and the educated in the middle, and the lowest level comprising the rural workers and manual labourers. Now, the system under a socialist government is far more egalitarian and there should be no social classes. Everybody is expected to work and contribute to the wealth of the country. Even children help out in family businesses or take on odd jobs after school.

In reality, there are still those who are richer or poorer than their fellow men. Increasingly, the city people are seen as having access to wealth and education while the farmers remain poor. Those who struggle to make a living cannot afford to observe many of the traditions or demonstrate the cultured behaviour of the wealthier, educated people. History has also had its effects and those who were seen as being on the side of the Southern forces during the Vietnam War have spent years in re-education camps. Upon their release, they have had limited access to the better-paying jobs or a higher level of education, compared with those who supported the North.

Status and Status Symbols

A person's identity derives from his family and its social standing, as well as from his religion, class and occupation. Traditionally, the Vietnamese are not a materialistic people. This is upheld by both Buddhism and communism, which endorse a frugal way of life. Few possessions are still needed but, increasingly, a television set and radio are now regarded as necessities. As foreign influences leave their impact, status symbols such as large houses are becoming more important but for most people, a motor scooter, karaoke set or video equipment scores maximum points with the neighbours.

Dress Standards

Until about 45 years ago, most working women wore long, dark-coloured sarongs as daily wear. The traditional outfit for a woman is

The ao dai *is the traditional dress for Vietnamese women.*

the *ao dai*. It has been modified over time from Chinese court clothing. Raglan sleeves were adopted in the 1930s according to the wishes of the emperor of the time, but the communists preferred the sturdy, working clothes of the peasant. The *ao dai* went out of vogue in the north in 1954 and in the south in 1975. Recently, it has made a comeback and is now regaining its popularity in the south among schoolgirls and office workers, and for formal functions.

To Western eyes, the *ao dai* is a very elegant and demure, yet sexy outfit. Long, wide-legged trousers are worn under a high-necked, long-sleeved, fitted tunic which is split on either side to just below the bust-line, allowing glimpses of bare midriffs. The pants should reach the sole of the feet and often just trail along the ground. The dress tunic has evolved according to fashion and has grown shorter and shorter until it now falls just below the knees. It can have the traditional mandarin-style collar or a boat-line one. Young girls wear only pastel colours or white but married women wear darker or brighter shades of tunic over white or black trousers.

Men used to wear a mandarin-like suit but this is rarely seen now except in traditional dance or music performances. Their tunic was shorter and much fuller than the *ao dai*. The colour was determined in the past by the class and rank of the person. For instance, purple denoted a high-ranking mandarin and blue, a lower-ranking one. Certain embroidered symbols were also an indication of these. Rural workers wear a practical, loose-fitting cotton top over dark trousers. They rarely wear shoes or sandals as these are impractical in the rice fields. Both sexes wear a wide-brimmed, conical hat to protect against the sun or rain.

In general, the people dress conservatively. Some young women wear figure-hugging, Western-style clothing but it is considered inappropriate to wear off-the-shoulder or revealing clothes during the day. Dress standards are also seen as an indication of social standing. The *ao dai* is worn by women who work as shop assistants or who are of a higher social status, but manual workers wear a loose top and baggy pants called an *ao ba ba*. A foreigner teaching English here was told to tuck her shirt into her trousers if she expected the students to respect and like her. It was pointed out that uneducated workers may leave their shirts billowing untucked and cooling their backs as they work, but this was inappropriate for the educated.

Similarly, shorts are only for male labourers and children, or for sports. Baggy black pants are traditionally worn by widows. Western-style fashions are becoming common and these can break the traditional rules of clothing as long as they are smart! The Vietnamese make it a point to dress up for formal occasions and even the children are carefully attired.

Health Care

Until recently, health care was widely available under an excellent free system and access to doctors, nurses and midwives was possible for most villagers as well as city dwellers. But fees have been imposed and while the poor are supposed to be exempt (with a certificate from their local authority), access to good care is no longer available to all. Equipment is old and of a poor standard. While most doctors were well-trained in the past, they have not been able to go for further training or update their knowledge. Those in government service are poorly paid and many have been forced into private practice. If a

person goes to hospital, a family member will usually stay with them, not just for emotional support, but also to help care for them, provide meals and pay for treatments if necessary.

The government has emphasised immunization coverage, improved hygiene and provided education on the prevention of diseases. It also promotes a longer period of breastfeeding to help cut the incidence of malnutrition and infant mortality. After analysing the devastating effects of chemicals such as Dioxin used during the Vietnam War, which appears to have resulted in excessive numbers of birth defects, there is now greater awareness of health risks. Much emphasis is placed on birth control (to help decrease the high rates of abortions). The incidence of drug abuse and sexually transmitted diseases such as AIDS is also closely monitored.

Traditional Cures

Traditional medicinal cures are as well respected as Western-style medicine and treatments. Because of the 1,000 years of domination by the Chinese, Vietnamese traditional cures are very similar to, but not always the same as, the much better-known Chinese ones.

The marks left from cupping, or *giac hoi*, and moxibustion, or *cao gio*, are often witnessed by visitors. Cupping, to draw out "bad wind" from an affected area, involves heating a small glass cup and placing it against the skin with the open side inwards. This creates a vacuum against the skin which breaks the small blood vessels in the surrounding area. It leaves multiple reddish circles and is often done on a person's back. Moxibustion relieves colds, flu or chest pains and involves rubbing the skin with a spoon or coin, leaving small bruises.

Herbal remedies, ointments, massages and acupuncture are also used to help maintain the balance between the *am,* the female or *ying* component, and the *duong,* which is the male or *yang* component. Illness is believed to be caused by an imbalance between the two. Of the 6,000 plants listed as growing in Vietnam, over 1,000 are noted as having medicinal properties.

RELIGION AND TRADITIONAL CUSTOMS

The Vietnamese way of viewing life has been strongly shaped by the people's religions and beliefs, and the result can be radically different from the Western perspective. As people age, instead of feeling sad at their physical decline, the elderly become content and have increased status in society. The Buddhists believe that a person's soul is not tied to the physical body and death is not final as the soul is reincarnated. Because of this, time is not a linear concept to the Vietnamese, but is viewed as cyclical. There is always another time and another day, year or life. In the West, the pursuit of happiness is something that people strive for. The Vietnamese, however, feel that they are born with it and one of life's most important tasks is to protect that happiness so that they will not lose it.

The religions of Vietnam are varied and rarely clear-cut. While some people call themselves Buddhists, it is likely that they also practise Confucian and Taoist principles, ancestral worship and a little animism, and are superstitious as well. Actual beliefs have developed over centuries from a melting pot of many ideas.

Traditional Vietnamese customs are an amalgamation of religious beliefs and old practices. They differ between areas and ethnic groups. Some customs, like commemorating the death anniversary of a person, stem from ancestral worship. These days, however, the younger generation prefers to celebrate birthdays. As one old man said, his children like to receive their presents now and see no reason to wait until they are dead!

A brief description of each of the main religions follows. The greatest emphasis is placed on Buddhism as it is the religion of approximately two-thirds of the population. Few would be regarded as devout, compared with believers in other countries, but the influence of Buddhism has strongly shaped the people's psyche.

Religion has also been tied to politics for many years. Some groups which were politically active, such as the Hoa Hao, were banned or found their ability to practise curtailed severely. While religious freedom is now accepted within the country, there are still problems importing religious material or proselytising.

Buddhism

Buddhist followers believe in the four noble truths spelled out by Buddha, or "The Enlightened One", who lived in India in the sixth century B.C. These are: that all lives experience suffering; suffering is caused by desire; suffering ceases when desire is eradicated; and suffering can be destroyed by adopting the "noble eight-fold path". This path includes having the right views; right thought; right speech (honesty); right conduct (including avoiding immoral acts, particularly the taking of life of any animal); right livelihood (not causing harm to others); right effort; right awareness of the past, present and future; and right contemplation (meditation).

These beliefs greatly affect the daily life of followers. While you may have no qualms about squashing a cockroach, believers will simply ignore the insect, or pick it up and place it outside. This may seem ludicrous as it is highly likely to find its way back in but the people believe it is wrong to kill any animal.

The wonderful variety of vegetarian food found in restaurants is also the effect of widespread Buddhism. Photos or prints of pin-up girls are not encouraged. It is regarded as a manifestation of personal impurity and is a weakness that should be avoided.

Buddhism has helped create a group of people who are gentle and tolerant. In some ways, it fits well with the communist ideology as it does not promote competition or value wealth. Followers should simply ensure that they have enough with which to get by. Buddhism also extols a great love for the environment and appreciation of other aesthetic areas. Norman Lewis, in *A Dragon Apparent,* tells of stories of mandarins paying for white herons to be released across the sky after the guests were seated in readiness to watch this spectacle. Caged birds are often seen on sale in the cities, not to be kept as pets, but for followers to buy and release, thus earning them extra merit in

A Buddhist monk praying in Tran Quoc Pagoda in Hanoi.

life. The cynic would point out that the purchase of the birds provides additional demand for the hunters to catch more birds from the wild, but this logic does not seem to worry the Buddhists.

There are three main sects of Buddhism in Vietnam. The largest sect is Mahayana. It developed in China and Japan and is strongest in the north. The second sect is a purer form called Theravada which came to Vietnam via the Khmers and is found mostly in the south. The smallest is Mendicant, which was founded relatively recently by a Vietnamese in the south.

A Buddhist pagoda has an abbot, or bonze, who oversees the work as well as the monks and nuns attached to it. Sickly children are sometimes given into the care of these Buddhists, who have a reputation of being able to heal and strengthen people, besides providing a high standard of education. Helping the poor, and taking in orphans and homeless children, is an important role of the monks and nuns. They do not have to stay in this role all their life, but may leave and marry if they wish.

Pagodas and statues can be seen everywhere throughout the country, as can the monks and nuns who are associated with them. You will be welcome to visit any pagoda or chat with the believers but there are a few niceties to observe. It is polite to introduce yourself to the abbot first and request permission to enter the pagoda. Always take your shoes off before you enter. Leave a small tip in the donations box. This money is spent on the upkeep of the pagoda. Pagodas are very busy at certain times. During regular Sunday school sessions, a monk helps educate people in the teachings of Buddha. At different times in the lunar calendar, followers visit the pagoda to pay homage (see Chapter 7). Monks and nuns follow a strict vegetarian diet. Followers visit the pagoda on special days and consume vegetarian food. These days vary between sects but are usually observed on the full-moon day in the middle and at the end of each lunar month.

Buddhism has been far more successful than Catholicism, not only because it has been present much longer, but also because it is more closely linked to Vietnamese traditions. Converts to Christianity have had to forgo their beliefs in ancestral worship and in the many ghosts, demons and gods that the Vietnamese deal with, whereas Buddhism can be blended with these other beliefs.

Hoa Hao

Scholars argue whether this is a sect of Buddhism or one which simply developed from its beliefs. Huynh Phu So lived in the Mekong delta and founded the movement in 1939 after being cured of illness. He

71

was known as the "mad monk" by the French but is believed to have about 1.5 million followers. His teachings espouse a simple form of worship that eliminates the need for intermediaries. The group was active politically and militarily, which resulted in its leader being put to death and the sect being banned.

Taoism

There are few pure Taoists living in the country but the ideas have permeated into the superstitions and beliefs of the people. Taoism originated in China and extols virtue, non-violence, compassion and humility. It has blended with old animistic beliefs to explain the mystical connections between heaven and earthly objects, and how these may influence a person through magic.

Confucianism

Rather than being a full-fledged religion, this is more a code for daily living. Confucius (Khong Tu), a Chinese born in 550 B.C., drew up a code of ethics to guide people in the areas of family, society and state. A person's class is decided by nature (or heaven) but once he is born, his actions determine his destiny. Confucianism places strong emphasis on duty, courtesy and virtue. It reinforces the respect given to teachers and elders and acts to strengthen family ties, heavily influencing daily social interactions.

Because a person's actions determine his future, much emphasis is placed on education. Schooling is widely available and learning is prized not only as a path to virtue, but also because it will increase a person's social status and power. Vietnam's high literacy rates are partly due to Confucianist traditions. Poetry is enjoyed by many, with friends composing short pieces for each other.

Ancestral Worship

This is very important in the lives of the Vietnamese, no matter which religion they purport to follow. Its origins stem from before any of the great religions arrived in the country, and elements are now blended with Buddhism and Confucianism. The Vietnamese have very strong family bonds that include the extended family and even the deceased. After a person dies, it is believed that his soul lives on to watch over and protect his descendants. The soul of the dead requires love and attention, say those who practise ancestral worship. Only then will the deceased be able to live on with the family, bless the members and even warn of impending disasters through dreams. If the soul is neglected, however, it becomes lost and lonely and has to wander around in the Kingdom of the Dead.

On the anniversary of a person's death, ceremonies are held in his memory. He is also remembered during the numerous lunar festivals and his soul is consulted during any important occurrence in the family—such as a birth, wedding or sickness—as if he were still alive. This can be done through the family altar. To maintain their connection with their ancestors, people often have a plot of family land which houses the ancestral burial grounds.

The land gives a sense of security and stability. The people live off the land and it provides a sacred bond between the present and past. The income from the ancestral land is used to support the ancestors and a male descendant is given the responsibility of ensuring that proper care is taken of it. So many families that have moved from the rural areas to the city have left a brother or son behind to care for the ancestors. Children are essential as they must care for the ancestors but the birth of a son is of additional importance as it is required that a male descendant look after the dead and oversee the worship of his ancestors. According to custom, a daughter or female descendant cannot do this. Evidence of such ancestral worship can also be seen in most pagodas, where there may be rows of old photographs of deceased people.

Because of the mass movements that occurred as Catholics moved south after North Vietnam came under communist rule in 1954, many of these ancestral links were destroyed. More recently, the push towards urbanisation has meant that a senior male family member must be left behind to look after the ancestral land and ensure that it stays in the family, while the others migrate to the city to seek their fortune. The observance of ancestral worship is so strong that most Catholics have a shrine for the dead in their house and even pray to it in what is called the Communion of Saints.

Christianity

Christianity is present in two main forms: Roman Catholicism, brought by the missionaries of Spain, Portugal and France from the 16th century, and Protestantism, which arrived more recently, in 1911. The latter is the smaller group, having only several hundred thousand followers, mostly among the hill tribes in the central highlands and some of the southerners influenced by the Americans.

Catholics constitute 8–10% of the population and, unlike Buddhism, the followers practise a fairly pure version of the belief. But their fortunes have waxed and waned in the country according to the politics of the time. Because the religion was firmly associated with European intervention in the country, particularly that of the French, its followers have been heavily persecuted. After communist rule was established in North Vietnam in 1954, a large number fled south and most are now concentrated around the outskirts of Ho Chi Minh City.

Islam

Muslims make up about 0.5% of the population and are mostly ethnic Khmers or Chams. Mosques can be seen in major towns and cities in south and central Vietnam. Islam originally arrived with the Arab traders and the form practised in Vietnam is not pure but has been blended with animism and Hinduism.

Cao Daism

This is a sect that developed in the 1920s, resulting in a very peculiar blend of religious beliefs and the veneration of saints. Its leader, Ngo

Minh (Van) Chieu, wanted to blend all the faiths in Vietnam together under a supreme being, the Cao Dai. Ideas from Buddhism, Confucianism and Taoism, together with Christianity, Islam and ancestral worship, were adopted. The range of saints includes Joan of Arc, Louis Pasteur, Victor Hugo, Napolean Bonaparte and other equally diverse characters. A single eye surrounded by the sun's rays is the group's key symbol. There are approximately two million followers centred around the group's colourful headquarters in Tay Ninh, northwest of Ho Chi Minh City.

Animism and Other Beliefs

Most Vietnamese, regardless of their religion, believe in the existence of spirits. These dwell in both living and non-living objects such as trees, kitchens, caves and mountains and must be kept happy. Literally hundreds of superstitions and ceremonies have evolved from this. For instance, if business is poor, a Vietnamese may burn a piece of paper to scare away the evil spirits causing the problems (see Chapter 7, Socialising in Vietnam). Astrology, geomancy and numerology also play a vital role in everyday life. People believe that the stars in the sky determine life's outcomes as much as human endeavours do.

Ghosts can appear in human form and then vanish. Great respect is paid to them as it is believed that they can reach into a person's chest and pull out his heart and soul. The people believe that there are many restless souls wandering around because of the numbers who died fighting the Vietnam War.

Black magic is still practised widely, particularly in the areas of business and love. For instance, if you are building a house and do not treat the construction team well during this period, they may put a "jinx" on the building. The Chams and Khmers are thought to have strong magical powers but religious mediums can be hired to help you achieve your desire or free you from another person's spell. Only those of strong minds, such as Buddhist monks, are thought to be immune to the magic.

Chapter Four

SETTLING DOWN

Your life in Vietnam will be as enjoyable and rewarding as you choose to make it. For many foreigners, settling in is quite a smooth process. It has its little hiccups but these can be minimised by making yourself aware of the situation in the country. Read Chapter 5, Culture Shock to help this process.

There are literally thousands of things that you should know about your new home in Vietnam before you arrive. Outlined here is an overview covering most of those things. Vietnam is changing so quickly—in terms of availability of goods, taxation, import-export rules and the bureaucracy concerning foreign residents—that too much detail would make the book out of date before it is even printed. The topics here will guide you on those areas in which you may want more specific information.

The majority of foreigners live in Ho Chi Minh City, Vung Tau (a day trip from Ho Chi Minh City) or Hanoi, so this book focuses on the living conditions in these cities. The situation in small towns or the more rural areas is basically the same, but there is far less choice in housing, nightlife and shopping. Remember also that Ho Chi Minh City is far more cosmopolitan than the rest of the country, so traditional values and practices may not be as evident there.

Perhaps the main point to remember is that foreigners appear to be wealthy. Do not flaunt your belongings. Not only is it frowned upon by the communist government, but frugality is also preached by the Buddhists and as Vietnam is one of the poorest nations in the world, it is simply not appropriate to display wealth in an ostentatious manner. Reminders come in many forms. A family in Vung Tau stocked their food cupboards on regular trips to Ho Chi Minh City as the choice is wider there and the prices, a little cheaper. Their landlord, on a house inspection, was shocked to see so much food and insisted to the family's maid that she help herself to the cans of food as the couple had far too much. It seemed indecent to the landlord that anyone could possibly hoard to such an extent. The maid, fortunately, had the sense to check with her employers first and the employers were, in turn, aghast at the suggestion.

THINGS TO KNOW BEFORE YOU ARRIVE

A little preparation in advance of the move may help you avoid many of the pitfalls along the way. Read what you can on Vietnam, including this chapter, so that you are familiar with the health issues, can make accurate importation lists for Customs and insurance, and can successfully plan what you need to bring with you and what you should leave behind.

Health

Health and medical care are important issues in Vietnam as these are not readily available within the country. The likely health problems will vary depending on your occupation, length of stay, location, budget and lifestyle. Make yourself aware of the main tropical diseases and illnesses that can occur in Vietnam, how they are spread and the symptoms of each. Update your own first-aid knowledge by taking a comprehensive course before you arrive. Always try to minimise the health risks.

Before Coming

Before you arrive, you should undergo a complete medical and dental checkup. Have your doctor provide sufficient supplies of any prescriptions that you require, or get a list of substitutes that are acceptable. There are chemist shops in Ho Chi Minh City and Hanoi, but you should ensure that the drugs you buy are packaged so you can check the brand, read the chemical composition and the expiry date.

Discuss with your doctor what vaccinations you should have. Different countries provide slightly different advice. Generally, Hepatitis A and B, diphtheria, tetanus, typhoid (vaccine or oral drug), Japanese encephalitis, meningococal meningitis, rubella, tuberculosis and an oral polio vaccine are considered necessary. An anti-rabies shot is also recommended for people in remote locations or those in a high-risk category. Other jabs may also be necessary depending on your own situation. Finally, bring overseas medical records with you to help new doctors keep track of your medical history.

Illnesses to Avoid

Diseases transmitted by mosquitoes, specifically malaria, dengue fever and filariasis, are prevalent. Some people choose to take prophylactic drugs to reduce their chances of contracting malaria but be aware that none of these offer absolute protection against the disease, nor do they prevent you catching other diseases that are transmitted by mosquitoes. The best method of prevention is to avoid being bitten. Also, the long-term use of these drugs can have serious side effects and these should be considered and discussed with your doctor. Use mosquito repellents, wear long-sleeved clothes and trousers during the evenings, make use of mosquito nets if your bedroom is not air-conditioned and avoid wearing dark-coloured clothing, perfumes and colognes during the evening as all these are known to attract mosquitoes.

Tuberculosis is also a threat and the disease is usually transmitted by the cough droplets of infected people or, less commonly, by drinking unpasteurised milk from infected cows. Fresh milk is currently untreated and is not recommended because of the wide range of bacteria that it can carry.

Sexually transmitted diseases are common and precautions should be taken. AIDS, known locally by its French name of SIDA, is on the increase as in most countries and condoms should be used. While these can be purchased locally, however, they are of poor quality.

Hygiene and Water

Be careful what you eat and watch the standard of hygiene at the places where you eat. To be safe, consume only foods that have been cooked thoroughly at a high temperature. All water should be boiled for at least 10–20 minutes to sterilise it, but bottled water appears to be of good quality, safe and can be bought in bulk. Water sterilisation tablets are fine for travelling but most people prefer not to use them over a long period. Ensure that the ice you have is made from boiled water or, if you cannot be sure, avoid it.

Do not eat raw vegetables and seafood, particularly from restaurants where hygiene is questionable. Peel fruit to avoid contamination from the skin. If you are on the street and feel thirsty but slightly unwell, one of the best drinks to settle a bad stomach and keep you hydrated is fresh coconut juice. The fruit is readily available all year round, everywhere in the country. Have the seller slice the top off a

79

green coconut and drink directly from the small hole that is created. This way, there is no chance of contamination from a glass or straw and the vitamins and minerals are excellent for you.

Acclimatisation

Help your body acclimatise. If you are moving from a cooler climate to a warmer one, it can place severe strains on the body.

Be sensible and take things slowly at first. Exercise will help keep you healthy, but confine it to the cool of the early morning or late afternoon and evening. Increase the amount of water you drink. Dehydration is a major problem even for those who do little exercise. An increased consumption of several litres of water a day is not too much. Prevention is certainly better than a cure in a country such as this. If you feel drained and tired, check your water, vitamin and mineral intake. Not all foods grown quickly in the tropics are high in nutritional value and you may not be eating a balanced diet.

Vitamin and mineral supplements are not readily available in Vietnam and it is advisable to take with you some multivitamins at least and, perhaps, oral electrolyte replacements that will help boost your body and health when you are not eating properly or feeling rundown from the all-too-common diarrhoea.

Accidents

Traffic accidents, snakebites, coral cuts and other problems requiring medical treatment can occur, with the first causing the greatest number of problems by far for foreigners. Everyone should take along a comprehensive first-aid kit and keep it handy. An example can be found in the Resources chapter.

Medical Treatment

Hospitals exist in most parts of the country but their facilities are limited. Many of the doctors have received little recent training and the equipment (where it exists) is outdated. There is a shortage of disposable items, so make sure you have needle-syringe combinations and equipment for bandaging and stitching cuts and abrasions. Foreign doctors practise in Ho Chi Minh City, Vung Tau and Hanoi (see Resources chapter for contacts) and some of the local doctors speak either French or English and are well-trained.

Depending on what is wrong with you, traditional Vietnamese medicine, as opposed to Western medicine, is readily available. It is similar to Chinese medicine and some aspects of it, such as acupuncture, are finding acceptance by Western-style doctors.

It is strongly recommended that all visitors be covered by medical insurance and join a medical assistance scheme. If you become seriously ill or suffer an accident, very little can be done for you within Vietnam. Companies such as AEA International and International SOS operate within the country, providing foreign doctors and nurses who can stabilise your condition and arrange medical evacuation for treatment. This is usually to Singapore, as it has the best range of acute-care facilities in the Asia Pacific region, or sometimes to Bangkok or Hong Kong. The companies also provide medical support for less life-threatening situations within Vietnam.

A medical insurance scheme alone may not be sufficient as none currently has representatives in Vietnam to deal with the problems, and local hospitals can be very reluctant to release a patient who needs evacuation to better facilities, probably because of pride and the loss of income. Always carry with you a first-aid kit and information on who to contact for emergency evacuation should the need arise. This should be translated into Vietnamese if it is to receive immediate attention.

To assist in evacuation procedures, ensure that you possess a valid visa and exit permit and that all necessary travel documents, or photocopies of these, are kept in a central location that is known to your senior management or someone whom the authorities would contact.

Clothing to Bring

Vietnam stretches over a long distance from north to south and the climate varies correspondingly (see Chapter 1). Bring loose-fitting, natural fibres for the south as they are most comfortable in the constant heat and humidity. Both summer and winter clothes are required for Hanoi in the north. Wherever you are, some of the new hotels or restaurants have the air-conditioning turned up to icy cold and a thin jacket can help prevent chills as you walk from the outside warmth into the cold inside. Do not forget clothes for the rainy season. In the south, the rain is often torrential and a good raincoat and suitable shoes are essential. Drycleaning is available in the larger cities only.

Business dress is usually neat but not too formal. Conservative clothes are preferred so for the men, for instance, a short- or long-sleeved shirt, dark trousers and tie will get them through most occasions. Most people lead a fairly active social life, creating their own fun with dinner parties and charity functions. Few of these are formal functions and a smart shirt for a man, and a dress or blouse and skirt for a woman, will be good enough for most evenings. If you are in the country for a long-term stay and like to dress up, take along the tuxedo and ballgown, but you will get to use these only a couple of times a year. In the evening, many people entertain outdoors or on roof-top gardens, and long sleeves and long trousers help protect against mosquito bites.

For daily wear, Hanoi is cooler and more formal and jackets are needed there, but they are rarely worn in Ho Chi Minh City because of the heat. Cool, comfortable fabrics such as a cotton-weave are best for the times when you are walking or sweltering in a warm car. Baggy black pants are traditionally worn by widows, although a pair of black trousers as part of an evening outfit is quite acceptable. The locals are not used to seeing women wearing skimpy clothes in public and shorts, low necklines and exposed shoulders will cause you to be hassled. Keep these clothes for home use, a private pool or a friend's house, and only if you have your own transport.

The variety of clothing that can be purchased in Vietnam is increasing but there are still problems for larger-sized people. Tailors can produce anything quickly and cheaply but few fabrics of good quality, apart from silk, linen or thicker cottons, are available. So if you plan to have your clothes tailored, bring the fabric with you. Take along plenty of underwear as well as it seems to deteriorate rapidly in the wash! Shoe quality is very poor there is little choice and large sizes are hard to find.

Shopping for Other Items

Vietnam is racing ahead in terms of shopping and every week a new item can be found on the grocery or shop shelves. Still, there are many personal items that are unobtainable. Medication, favourite brands of cosmetics, books, children's games or things such as car restraint seats for children have to be brought in with you.

Most household items such as refrigerators, freezers, washing machines, stereos, television sets and generators can be found. But some household items such as decent cutlery, good-quality crockery and a good can opener are virtually unobtainable. Upholstery fabrics and shower curtains can be difficult to find in the right colour and of the quality and price you may prefer. Supply is improving but is often intermittent and highly priced, or the goods are made locally and the quality is questionable. There is a constant flow of expatriates in and out of the country and you can often ask an obliging friend to pick up for you items from Singapore, Kuala Lumpur, Bangkok or Hong Kong.

ARRIVING IN VIETNAM

Customs

All rules, taxes and regulations change rapidly so check carefully to ensure that your information is up to date. You will need to obtain a visa prior to your arrival. When you enter, there is the usual round of paperwork. The first time you enter, a passport photo is needed for the Immigration Department's files. It is best to have several of these with you, as extras always seem to be used up quickly. You must declare all goods such as computers, electronic equipment and camera gear, as well as cash and credit cards. Taxes have been imposed on incoming household shipments and the tax on second-hand items is higher than that on new goods (to encourage you to buy there instead).

In addition to these items, Customs officials check all goods brought into the country, whether by air or sea. Imported antiques need to be registered if you want to be able to take them with you when you leave. These will have a label pasted on them that cannot be removed prior to your departure. All pornography and politically-oriented material is banned. Videos, compact disks, cassettes, books, and computer disks are taken for censorship. This usually takes two to three weeks and all approved items are returned to you in good order. However, it is not advisable to bring anything irreplaceable, as things have been known to go missing. Censorship can be quite wide-ranging and movies such as the James Bond series are not permitted into the country because of the East versus West theme. Inadmissible material can be stored in a warehouse here (at a small cost) until you leave, or you can have it redirected to another country.

The regulations are changed periodically. If you can, visit the country first, see what is available, check the latest rules through a reliable removal company operating there and then arrange to have your air or sea shipment packed and sent.

To help streamline the Customs process, it is a good idea to draw up a list of everything in your shipment. Include the titles, authors and singers of all your books, music cassettes and compact disks. Serial numbers and power ratings for all electrical items—mostly stereos and television sets, videos, computers and other electronic items—are required. This list is worth doing properly as it can be used for insurance purposes too. The same rules apply if you are carrying goods in by hand. Only one television or video set can be brought in duty-free. If you have a second set for a bedroom, you will have to pay import tax on it.

Of course, as in any place in the world, there can still be unexpected delays. One Egyptian found himself detained by Immigration and quizzed by a curious official on the subject of the pyramids for over half an hour. Wedding and baby photos always seem to slow down Customs searchers as they admire them and check who is who in the family photos. Luckily, as more people arrive, the procedure is getting smoother and faster.

Good Buys Within Vietnam

Good-quality rattan furniture is available at reasonable prices and most people use this to furnish their houses. Carpentry is also of a good standard but you need to check that the wood has been fully dried first as there can be problems with warping. Antiques are readily available but cannot be taken out of the country. There is no strict definition of what constitutes an antique and anything over 40 years old may be classified as one. Ivory and tortoiseshell items are protected species, although they are commonly on sale. While you may not have difficulty taking it out of Vietnam, you are likely to face stiff fines and confiscation of the material upon your arrival home, depending on your destination, because of the Convention for International Trade in Endangered Species (CITES) regulations.

Lacquerware, ceramics and painting have long been techniques that the Vietnamese excel in. Ceramics and lacquerware are now mass-produced and exported to all parts of the world. Vietnamese art is beginning to be discovered by the world art market. Contemporary art may be in any style and medium but silk painting and woodcut block prints are the traditional art forms. Mother-of-pearl inlay is produced with painstaking care to make many fine pieces of furniture, pictures or ornaments. Amber, jade and gemstones such as rubies and sapphires can be made into jewellery relatively cheaply. Fine embroidery, stone carvings and silk are all good buys.

Shophouses in Hanoi offer a range of local goods and services, but imported products are generally hard to find.

Bargaining

Virtually everywhere, bargaining is the usual means of determining a price—whether it is for a cyclo ride, or to buy a dress, refrigerator or mango. Increasingly, in some of the tourist places, a fixed-price system is emerging. Bargaining is much tougher than in many other parts of Asia and the discount you are likely to get varies enormously depending on what you are buying and where, and how long you spend haggling over the price. For regular items such as food, you will probably pay the same prices as locals do. If you think you are being ripped off, do not buy, but check with a Vietnamese friend first on how much you should pay. That person will let you know a fair price.

HOUSING

Looking for accommodation is time-consuming and expensive, but some beautiful old villas or smaller central apartments are available. Slowly, more properties are coming onto the rental market but the choice is still very limited, particularly in the shorter term, so some people stay in hotels for months at a time. Suites are available in some hotels at reasonable prices and it is worth shopping around and inspecting as many rooms and facilities as possible before you decide where to stay. While putting up in a hotel may seem luxurious, the novelty soon wears off. Space can be quite limited and eating out for every meal becomes tiring.

Service apartments are starting to come into the market and these are a logical alternative for working people. While such apartments seem expensive initially, living in a house is not much easier on the pocket because of high costs and what appears to be an endless string of problems. A centrally located service apartment can be the ideal choice for an individual or couple who do not require much space.

The quality of housing is variable and there are many things to keep in mind when you go house-hunting. Generally, two types of properties exist: restored villas (or unrestored ones that you can renovate to your own taste) and "tunnel houses"—tall, skinny towers built on a small road frontage to minimise land tax. Real estate agents, most of whom are attached to service companies, are available to help you search. Standards vary enormously. Many show you what is available rather than what you have specifically asked for. They also take a hefty commission, so enquire about this first.

You may be in Vietnam to take up a post in an existing company but, just as often, others arrive on their own looking for business opportunities or trying to set up a branch office for an overseas company. Finding office accommodation involves many of the same problems as searching for a home. Business centres exist in both Ho Chi Minh City and Hanoi as an interim measure or as a longer-term solution. Fax and telephone charges can be expensive, though.

What to Look For

There are many things to bear in mind when searching for a house. Entertaining is often done at home and, if you intend to hold dinner parties, you will have to consider whether the kitchen and dining areas are large enough for your purpose. Then there are other considerations as well. For example, is there sufficient living space? Is there room for a billiards or table-tennis table?

You will probably have house guests and may have to provide accommodation for other people within your company when they visit. Domestic help and security guards are common and you may also have a driver as well. Will the staff be living in? Your living areas must be completely separate from the staff's so you can lock up at night. Is there somewhere for them to relax when they wait for you, or space for the ironing to be done, out of your way, if you entertain guests during the day?

Even if the staff do not live on the property, they need access to a bathroom, usually one that is separate from yours. The ease of living in the house and the privacy it affords can greatly affect your happiness in the country. Your house will be your sanctuary for the duration of your stay in Vietnam, so choose carefully within your budget.

Home Security

While break-ins are not common, they do occur and electronic goods or camera equipment are likely targets. Burglar alarms are rare and cannot be purchased in the country yet. If you bring one with you, be prepared to spend considerable time overseeing its installation.

Electricity

The infrastructure here varies enormously. Check the water supply, power and telephone lines carefully as they can be very expensive to alter. Power is a particular issue. Electricity in many houses has not been earthed and very old wiring is common. Blackouts are common in the dry season due to a reliance on hydro-electricity, and you may well need a generator (this can be noisy, so be careful where it is placed). Ask the neighbours about power cuts and any other problems they may encounter. Most people keep a variety of candles, oil lamps, matches and torches in each room, just in case they are needed suddenly.

The electricity in Vietnam is moving towards being standardised at 220V, 50 cycles, with round, two-pin or flat, three-pin plugs as the norm. Older houses may still be operating with 110V, but these are gradually being changed to 220V. You made need a step-up transformer, depending on which electrical appliances you want to run and how many other houses in your area get their electrical supply from the same line. Some people have their houses rewired and upgrade to three-phase power. To do this, you need a licence from the government and obtaining one can be quite a costly exercise. Major appliances and machines such as computers should be run through a voltage regulator or uninterrupted power supply to avoid their being damaged by the frequent sags and surges that occur. If you like cooking, gas ovens are preferable to electric ones for this same reason, besides being a cheaper form of power. There seems to be little comprehension about the dangers of combining water and electricity. There are instances of electrical outlets being installed in shower units right in the path of the water stream (so that one can shave and shower at the same time?). If you rent a house like this, insist that changes be made!

Water Supply

Water pressure needs to be tested carefully in each area of the house. Check the colour of the walls as the water pipes are usually cemented into these and many leak slightly, leaving stains on the walls and giving the room a musty smell. Make sure that the water pump is working well and is not too noisy. The average pressure in one house became very low after a few months and the washing machine took over six hours to run through a cycle. The problem was solved when the taps were removed. A discarded cigarette butt left in the pipes during construction had worked its way down to a single tap and blocked it. The washing machine whizzed through later loads in less than an hour!

Tap water is not suitable for drinking anywhere in Vietnam. It should be filtered and boiled for at least 10–20 minutes to make it drinkable or for it to be made into ice. Bottled water can be purchased easily. In Ho Chi Minh City, many people choose to have water delivered, and large bottles provide the supply for hot and cold water-dispensing machines.

Telephone and Communication Links

Check if a telephone has been installed in the house and if it has an International Direct Dialling (IDD) facility should you need it. You do not need IDD to receive overseas calls, only to make them. Getting a telephone line and an IDD facility can take several months and be very expensive. To get around this problem, mobile phones have become popular. However, this system is now becoming overloaded. Depending on the model, the range of mobile phones can also be quite limited. Pagers are becoming increasingly common in Hanoi and Ho Chi Minh City. Faxes require special permits that take time and money to obtain, as do modems. Be aware that all communication links are monitored by the government, so be careful what you say!

Noise and Space

Vietnamese suburbs are noisy. They start the day early and have not heard of noise pollution rules. Look at the area surrounding your future house carefully. Many streets are busy and vehicular noise can be very considerable early in the morning and during the evenings. Radio and television sets are turned on at a high volume. Loudspeakers emit broadcasts from many government establishments. As Vietnam is undergoing a rapid boom, construction noise and dust can be a problem. Check if any major works are near you. Back streets are usually quiet but very narrow and a car cannot easily be left on the side of the road without infuriating the neighbours. So if you have a car, you will need to provide parking space for it.

A house in a compound that has sports facilities may be worth considering if you have young children. It provides a relatively quiet area for them to wander and play in. Alternately, try to find a large garden as there are few public areas that children can use, and little after-school recreation is available. This also avoids the problem of the children being mobbed by friendly strangers each time they go outside.

Permission to Live There

Even after you have found the perfect house, the problems may not be over. All lease agreements must be approved by the government. For you to be able to rent, the foreign company that you work for must have an investment licence from the Ministry of Trade to conduct business in Vietnam, and a letter from the State Committee for Cooperation and Investment (SCCI) stating that you have a representative office licence, are awaiting the issue of a licence or have a letter of introduction from the People's Committee. Similarly, for a Vietnamese company or individual to rent a home to a foreigner, the party must have the appropriate licence from the Management of Real Estate Office (Department of Land and Housing), approval from the police and the architect's office, and a construction permit.

Costs

The terms of the rental contract are controlled by the state. A minimum rent has been set for all properties designated for foreigners. It is calculated according to the property's size. The landlord must pay tax on the rental income that he receives. Currently, 31% of the agreed rate goes jointly to the Ministry of Finance (25%) and the service company through which you signed the contract.

Rental costs tend to be very high in Hanoi and Ho Chi Minh City. Many landlords ask for a deposit of one month's rent while renovations or alterations are being done to the house and a year's rent in advance after that. Make sure that all alterations and the terms of the contract are in writing, including things such as the provision of a telephone for your sole use, and the provision of air-conditioners or ceiling fans. As renovations usually take longer than estimated, be careful about setting the actual date that rental payments should commence, or you will find yourself paying for your hotel bill as well as rent on an unfinished house. If you have agreed to pay for some or all of the renovations in return for a lower rental cost, it may be worth extending the number of optional years that the property may be rented at the fixed price stated in the contract.

Whether the renovations are being paid for by you or by the landlord, make sure you supervise the process carefully. Stories of doors being put in the wrong place three times, or of sub-standard workmanship, are all too common. Catch these mistakes as early as possible and insist that things be rectified.

As more houses are made available for rental, the terms are becoming increasingly negotiable. But this is offset by the fact that, with more foreigners arriving in Vietnam, the prices are tending towards an increase. In the beginning, most houses were rented unfurnished and the person who rented had to pay for any renovations. This is slowly changing and partially or fully furnished houses can be found now, with the landlord paying for part or all of the renovations.

DOMESTIC STAFF

Most foreign residents have some form of domestic help. Such help is relatively cheap and frees you to attend to other tasks. Some people hire a cook, maid, nanny, gardener and night security guard, depending on their needs. The cook and maid duties may be carried out by one person. You may also need a security guard and a driver.

Some people are used to having staff working in their house for

Unpacking household goods with the help of a domestic staff member.

them. For others, it is a foreign notion and takes quite a lot of adjustment. Household staff can fast become both your saviours and, at times, the bane of your life. The most important characteristics are honesty, trustworthiness and, above all, they must be compatible with your own personality. These people will be with you virtually every day of your time in Vietnam. You must be able to trust them with your possessions and get along with them. These issues are even more important than their ability to speak English, or how well they do their job.

Going back into history, household help was a familiar concept during French times and for centuries, wealthy Vietnamese families

93

employed household staff. During the years of communist rule, however, this concept was largely done away with. Today, with mothers in the workforce, the practice is again becoming more common, especially among the wealthier families, although members of the extended family often help with household chores. Presently, those who take up such domestic jobs view it with mixed emotions. Some look upon it as a good choice of work, paying a much better and more regular salary than do other jobs. Other Vietnamese, however, do not see it as socially acceptable and, while they may like the work and pay, do not want the nature of their job to be made known to others.

Ensure that your staff get on well together. A happy household works much better and there are fewer problems. The staff will work out their own pecking order and settle down. Always remember that it is your house and you are the boss. Tell them and teach them how you want things done and make it clear if something really bothers you. If you want them to follow a routine—for instance, to water the house plants every day—tell them so. They cannot read your mind and it is amazing how many things are done differently from place to place.

Some things must always be explained to your staff. Do not expect the maid to understand how to use a washing machine and the amount of detergent to use with it. Make it clear when, and how, you want the refrigerator and freezer cleaned. Discuss hygiene and emphasise the rule of food preparation, including the washing of hands before handling food. Do not assume that the staff know all these things.

Make it clear how you want money to be accounted for. The maid often shops at the market for fruits, vegetables, meats and various small items. Receipts are not available from these food stalls, so most people keep a running tally in a book showing the money given to the maid and an itemised list of what she has spent it on. Buy the odd item yourself occasionally and compare the price you have paid for it against what she has listed. This way, you let her know that you

Expatriates buying food at the local market.

are doing a spot check on the prices that she quotes you without appearing overly suspicious about the matter.

There are so many wonderful fruits and vegetables that it can be hard to explain what it is that you want the maid to buy. Take along an Asian cookbook that carries pictures of a variety of fruits and vegetables, and use these to help as a shopping guide. A butcher's diagram of meat cuts can also be useful to describe the piece you want. An English-Vietnamese cookbook exists for Western food. It is very basic but can be used as a starting point. When asking for Vietnamese dishes to be made, copy the names of your favourite dishes from a local Vietnamese restaurant and show this to your cook. You will enjoy the results.

Privacy is something that the Vietnamese respect naturally. If you take a siesta, let the staff know that you do not want to be disturbed.

Or, if you work from home and want your work area to be cleaned when you are out, inform them about it. They will quickly observe your routine and allow you your own space. Having done all this, you may find yourself coming home during the lunch break, only to see the maid stretched out on the ground floor, asleep. Before you lose your temper, stop and think. A siesta is common for many of the people and the floor is often the coolest place in the heat of the day. If work is left unfinished at the end of the day, then have a chat with the person concerned. Most maids and guards manage to fulfil all their daily tasks and snooze through the hottest part of the day.

Whether your staff live in with you or simply turn up for the hours they are required to work, you will need to provide some furniture for them. A small table and a chair each is normal so that they can sit and have a coffee or tea break during the day. You may choose to provide a small burner so that they can heat water themselves. By providing this furniture, you will also have designated where their rest area is to be. It should be out of the rain and within sight of your front gate as the security guards usually sit there.

Technically, you cannot hire staff directly, but must do it through a Vietnamese foreign service company. A substantial portion of what you pay goes to the company, and the remainder is the pay that your staff receives. The company will help you negotiate conditions such as salary, sick leave, holiday leave, maternity leave, and so on. These have to conform with the country's labour laws but the salary varies considerably, depending on whether or not you are also providing food and lodging for the staff. It is normal for them to have public holidays off, but many will work through these times if you need them and take time off in lieu at a later stage.

An additional month's salary is given to all employees just prior to Tet, the Vietnamese New Year, as an annual bonus. Overtime pay is commonly given if you have large parties or late nights that require guards and maids to do extra work and stay up later than usual. Festivals and public holidays are listed in Chapter 7, Socialising in

Vietnam and this also outlines other times when it would be appropriate to give gifts or do something special for your staff.

Problems

Communication is the biggest cause of misunderstandings and problems. Have shopping lists written down in both English and Vietnamese so that both you and the maid understand what is on it. If you give
directions for something to be done and the person nods and says
"yes", do not assume that he has understood. He is simply being polite
towards you. If he speaks English, get him to repeat what you have
said. If the matter is important, get someone who can translate for
you—the driver or, perhaps, a company secretary who can do it over
the phone. Many times, the employer tends to get angry, thinking that
the staff have been lazy and have not done what was required of
them. Almost always, this is due to miscommunication and is not
the result of laziness or bad habit.

Sometimes, you "inherit" staff along with a house provided by
your company. This often works well as it means one thing less for
you to do when you move in. Another plus point is that the staff are
already familiar with the jobs that have to be done around the house.
But problems can arise if they are not prepared to adjust to your way
of doing things, or if they believe they are employed by the company
and not by you, and so refuse to accept your directions. If this becomes
an issue, do something about it immediately.

It is widely accepted that you hire a new employee with a
probationary period attached to the job. If, during this time, you
discover that you really do not like him (or her), dismiss the person in
a civil manner and avoid making him "lose face". Always pay him off
immediately and ensure that he leaves your premises with all his
possessions (and none of yours or the company's) right away.

Hiccups aside, the staff are wonderful and allow you to have the
free time to enjoy the country and lead a busy social life. Household
chores vanish and you feel at home in the neighbourhood. Your staff

97

know what is happening in the local area and can alert you to a spate of break-ins, a disruption to your normal transport route due to a road being dug up, or warnings of power cuts in certain suburbs that are given in advance in the local newspapers. They can also fill you in on all the local gossip and answer your questions about the everyday things you notice as you drive around. They are crucial in determining your happiness in the country so if things are not as you would like them to be, take appropriate action.

PETS

It is generally kinder on your pet not to bring it to Vietnam, even though it may be heartbreaking to leave it with friends or to find another home for it. There are many diseases here that dogs and cats can succumb to and they may find the tropics difficult to adjust to. Gardens tend to be small and there is little room for them. On top of that, it is expensive to ship an animal and upon your return, there are frequently lengthy delays, high costs and the necessary quarantine. The animal may also be kidnapped and resold, or ransomed back to you within Vietnam. Dogs are usually bred to be eaten and it may be hard to get staff to care for the animal in your absence. Pets are seen as a burden and not a luxury.

Many people see their stay in Vietnam as a great opportunity to keep an exotic pet, such as a monkey or parrot. This is not recommended. Apart from supporting the animal trade which is decimating the native fauna, it is also difficult to care for these animals properly. They are susceptible to diseases which, in the case of monkeys, may be transferable to man and vice versa. Few vets know how to treat these animals. Also, most foreigners plan to work and live in Vietnam for a few years only. While the animal may have been cute as a baby, what are you going to do with it when you leave? Many native animals cannot be exported without special permits, which are very difficult to obtain. Few other expatriates want an animal dumped on them. The owners will then have to find a home for their pets when they leave.

Some people settle for a dog to act as both guard dog and pet. If you do this, take the animal to the veterinarian and ensure that it is given all the necessary injections.

MOVING IN

Establish a routine as soon as you can. This will help you and your family feel more at home. It will also allow your staff to develop a pattern of working that fits in with your schedule. Write down your new address or, better still, have a card made. Your pronunciation of Vietnamese words is often completely indecipherable to a taxi or cyclo driver and it is much easier to show them your address. You can also hand out the cards to friends so that they, too, can find your place. Cards are cheap to make. Have personal cards printed separately, apart from your business cards. You may want to include a map on the back to help friends find your place if you are likely to entertain at home.

When you first move in, there are several formalities that must be attended to. Take all the passports of the household residents with you to the local police station. This is often done together with the landlord. You must register the names of those who will be living in the house so that if there are any problems or accidents, the police will know who is in the area. If you have overnight visitors, they must also be registered, although many people do so only for guests who stay for an extended period.

Do not be surprised if several local people come and introduce themselves to you. This is particularly the case if you live in an area where there are few other foreigners, as you will be somewhat of a novelty. The people may simply want to practise their English, learn about you and your country or help you settle into Vietnam. This can be a great boon as they may be able to help translate instructions to your staff or answer questions that you may have. Sometimes, though, the friendliness can become a burden with people wanting to borrow money, use the telephone or watch your video. Decline all such requests as politely as possible. Also, let it be known when you can be visited so that people do not turn up at inconvenient times.

Your electricity and water bills are usually prepared monthly and delivered to the door for payment when the meter reader visits. Garbage collection also needs to be organised. Virtually everything is recycled here. Find out from your staff or neighbours what the usual arrangements in your area are.

CHILDREN

Issues tend to alter depending on the age of the child, as outlined in the children's section in Chapter 5, Culture Shock. Safety is a general concern for all ages, though. Many of the problems are related to the traffic and because of this, young children tend to be ferried around everywhere in cars. They do not go anywhere on their own so it is difficult to allow for the gradual development of independence.

Access to swimming pools and large play areas is also a problem. The larger hotels often offer sports facilities on a membership basis and while this is not cheap, it can be worthwhile.

Babies

Most baby-care items can now be bought within Vietnam. Health care and the fear of unknown viruses are the greatest of worries. There are few areas where you will be able to go outside and push a pram.

Toddlers and Pre-school

Play groups are popular and it is sometimes difficult to get a place in them. There are no established standards, so inspect them yourself and make sure that you are happy with the facilities and supervisors.

Primary Schoolchildren

Ho Chi Minh City, Vung Tau and Hanoi offer a few choices of schools but this is not so in other parts of the country (see Resources chapter for contact information). Some people prefer to teach their children at home but this will exclude regular interaction with other children. All the schools are small and most are made up of quite a mix of cultures. This can make it difficult for a child to find friends but there are enormous benefits from the cross-cultural learning experiences. Sports and extra-curricular activities are very limited but, again, other opportunities more than make up for this.

School times vary slightly from school to school. An example is the Ho Chi Minh City International School where the hours are from 7.50 a.m. to 2.30 p.m., Mondays to Fridays. Schools follow the European school calendar and the school year runs from August to June, with a break period of about 10 weeks in-between.

High-School Students

There is very little choice of establishments at high-school level and facilities are limited, but growing fast. Some people choose to live in Singapore with their children while one parent works in Vietnam and flies home each weekend, if possible. This is not always practical so others put their children into boarding school, with one parent taking regular flights home. Another choice is to sign up for correspondence courses. Well-structured programmes are available at a considerably lower cost than for the previous options. The family is also kept together and the child learns self-discipline.

SHOPPING FOR FOOD

Most of the shopping is done at the market. You can go there yourself or get the maid to do it. It is best to buy from such places early in the morning as there is no refrigeration. Products are brought in from the country very early in the day and you have the best choice of the freshest items then.

The vegetables, fruits, seafood and meats are generally excellent, although tender beef seems to be impossible to find locally. There is little fresh milk available and, because of health risks it is not recommended. Most people use ultra-heat-treated (UHT) imported milk and cream, or powdered milk. Thanks to the French influence, fresh bread is baked twice a day. In the north, it is made from wheat flour and in the south, from rice flour. It is good and crusty but only white bread is available and tends to have little flavour. Sweeter bread is also produced, but this is not to everyone's taste.

Small shops stocking Western-style foods are coming up. These can be expensive and goods may be kept beyond their expiry date. Alternatively, they may not always be in stock, depending on when the last shipment came in. People tend to store essential items or goods that are rarely seen. "Buy when you see, rather than when you want" is the general rule. Because of this, you will need a much larger refrigerator and freezer, as well as cabinet storage areas, than you normally would. Some shops have refrigeration now and this means that a wider range of cheese and dairy products are available than previously.

Shopping hours vary considerably but most places are open from early in the day until late in the evening, although they may close between 11.30 a.m. and 2.30 p.m. It is more likely, however, that the shop remains open through the heat of the day, but the staff are snoozing and you will have to wake them up to be served.

WEIGHTS AND MEASURES

The metric system is used here together with a Chinese system of measuring gold. Gold is always sold by the tael. One tael is equivalent to 37.5 grams. There are 16 taels to the catty, making it equivalent to 0.6 kilograms. Most expensive purchases, such as houses or land, are quoted and transacted locally in gold as large amounts of US dollars are unobtainable and the *dong* comes in small denominations and, until recently, suffered from inflation.

TRANSPORTATION

Bicycles and motor scooters dominated the streets until recent times. The few trucks and cars that have survived the roads have had very little maintenance but ingenious repairs have kept vehicular dino-saurs on the road well past their retirement age. In Ho Chi Minh City, the rapid increase in the number of cars and motorcycles has made the traffic a nightmare. Hanoi has fewer cars and is quieter but the streets are becoming increasingly busy.

Traffic accidents are very common as driving and road awareness skills have not increased correspondingly. Most foreigners do not drive, for their own and other road users' safety. Cars can be rented, with the services of a driver, and many people opt for this system. While not cheap, they can be shared and the driver can be sent on delivery errands which saves considerable time. A driver who speaks English and knows his way around the city is invaluable as he can be sent out to search for the more unusual items that you may need. If you are a passenger in an accident, it is usually better to let your Vietnam-ese driver sort it out and for you to disappear from the scene as soon as is practical.

Cyclos, rented motorcycles and bicycles are cheaper modes of transport. While helmets are not widely worn, they are strongly recommended. You can currently ride a motorcycle of less than 70 c.c. without a Vietnamese driver's licence. It is a handy and cheap way to get around town. For larger motorcycles, property ownership may be a problem. It can be registered in a Vietnamese friend's name or, if your company has a foreign representative's licence and you take the local driver's test, you can keep a motorcycle of up to 250 c.c. (larger bikes can no longer be bought in Vietnam). When you keep a motorcycle, you should be covered by insurance. You will have to pay for parking in the central areas but will be issued a ticket and receipt for this.

Horns are used and lights are flashed continuously to let others on the road know of your presence. Other road rules appear to be scanty. Cars must keep to the left lane, even when turning right. Everyone gives way to vehicles that are larger than their own.

Alternatively, use one of the motorcycle-taxis that hang out on

Cyclos are used extensively for short-distance transport.

street corners waiting for business. It is best to use the same driver as much as possible so you build up some form of trust and rapport. Be careful to keep the knees tucked in and if you are a woman, try not to put your arms around the driver to steady yourself as he may think that you are being forward! On cyclos or bikes, watch out for your valuables so they do not get snatched by motorcycle thieves.

Moving around the country is best done by plane. The road system is very bad and slow and, while the rides can be spectacular and are a great way to see the country, they take a long time. Most people prefer not to drive at night due to the high incidence of accidents. It is not always possible to find decent places at reasonable rates where you may stay overnight. A train service runs between Ho Chi Minh

City and Hanoi, making stops along the way and taking about 38 hours in all. First-class is quite cheap and comfortable but always keep a mesh screen over the window as children enjoy throwing rocks at passing trains, sometimes with horrific results. It also keeps hands out of your space when the train pulls up at stops and you may be asleep. Public buses do run from town to town but are crowded and usually non-air-conditioned. For a slightly higher price, a ticket on an air-conditioned mail bus can be purchased for some runs.

BANKING AND CURRENCY

The banking system has provided an unlimited source of frustration, bad jokes and tales for years but luckily, it is improving fast. A variety of international banks now have their offices in Ho Chi Minh City and Hanoi. Once you leave these centres, you need to use a local bank such as the State Bank and Vietcombank, or carry cash. Traveller's cheques can be cashed in banks but often with a very hefty fee and they may demand to see not only your passport, but the original purchase receipt as well. Credit cards are not widely accepted. Newer joint-venture hotels and restaurants tend to accept them, as do some large tourist shops. Do not rely on being able to pay by this means unless you have checked with the establishment first. Slowly, more places are starting to accept credit cards but they can be more of a hassle than what they are worth. One establishment refused to accept any credit cards that were not on the list they had been sent. The owner of the card gave up trying to explain that the list was actually of terminated or stolen cards that should be rejected!

Currently, payment in either U.S. dollars or the Vietnamese *dong* is acceptable in most establishments. The government is trying to discourage the use of US dollars but many people still prefer to use them. In the country, it is easier to carry large denominations of US currency as the largest *dong* note is only equivalent to about US$5. However, always carry at least small sums of *dong* to pay for cyclo rides or minor purchases.

Where possible, it is better to pay by *dong* as the exchange rate quoted by many shops or restaurants is not always attractive. Money-changers usually give a good rate (but check it each time) and are open from early in the day until late.

Torn or dirty foreign notes, including those with writing on them, will often be rejected, even by banks. Check those given to you as change. Request newer notes as you may not be able to use the older notes later on. When it comes to *dong* notes, some of them seem to have spent the last six months circulating on the floor of the fish market and, as no one would bother counterfeiting those, even the filthiest note is readily accepted. You will often be handed these as change as the giver will hope that you will screw up your nose at the sight of them and say "keep them".

There is no longer a significant difference between the official bank exchange rate and that available on the street. Currently, US$1 is equivalent to about 11,000 *dong*. *Dong* notes are in the denominations of 100, 200, 500, 1,000, 2,000, 5,000, 10,000, 20,000 and 50,000. Beware of the 5,000 and 20,000 notes as both are in a similar shade of blue and are easy to confuse. Transferring money into the country is a slow process, even when it is done through an international bank, so check how long it will take if you need the money urgently. Banking hours vary a little but are usually from 9 to 11 30 a.m. (local banks open at 7 a.m.) and from 1.30 to 3.30 p.m. Mondays to Fridays, and from 9 a.m. until noon on Saturdays.

POSTAL SYSTEM

The post is improving and letters usually take two to three weeks to arrive at their destination. All packages coming in or going out of the country have their contents examined by Customs, causing an additional delay. Not all packages or bulky letters, such as those containing photographs, reach their destination. It is better to post these from Singapore, Hong Kong or another country, if possible. Bring in stamps from one of these countries, together with the mailing costs by weight, so that you can hand a parcel or letter to a friend travelling out of Vietnam without feeling guilty about the associated costs or hassle. Many businesses have their post couriered in and out of the country to avoid these problems. Post is censored in the same way that all shipments are, so expect a delay on any videos, books, compact disks or tapes being sent in or out of the country.

When a parcel arrives for you, there will first be a letter of notification from the post office. Take this and your passport to the post office to claim your package, the contents of which will be opened and checked in front of you. Allow at least 30 minutes to an hour for this procedure.

Major post offices offer express post (via courier), fax, telex and telephone services. Fax machines are also available at major hotels or business centres. Stamps and envelopes do not usually come with an adhesive or glue on their backs and so you will need to use sticky tape or the glue provided by the post office to affix stamps and seal letters.

107

NEWSPAPERS AND BOOKS

There are several English-language newspapers and magazines printed within Vietnam. These cover local news and the business scene. Some international papers and magazines can be bought but the choice is quite limited. There is a listing of these in the Resources chapter.

Satellite dishes can be purchased and many hotels have these, allowing patrons to catch international news coverages as well as sports, soap operas and music videos. Short-wave radio is another popular means of staying in touch with international news.

Book supplies are very limited. There are a few books about Vietnam but the majority of novels are purchased outside the country and swapped from person to person once inside. Video tapes are available for rent but most are copies of poor quality.

TRAVELLING

Vietnam is a fascinating country and well worth taking a break from work to explore. There are several good travel guides (listed in the Resources chapter) to help you decide where to go and what to see. Police permits are needed only for the more remote regions. You will need to take your passport and entry-exit paper with you because each night you will have to register at the hotel or place where you stay.

There is a dual-pricing system for many tourist items. Locals pay a low price and you will pay a high one. This is true even for Vietnam Airline flights around the country, although this will be phased out shortly. It may seem unfair but to the Vietnamese, the practice reflects the disparity in wages and there is no way you can avoid paying the "official foreigners' price". But you can still bargain over unofficial high prices.

If you travel in a group and wish to tip the bus driver or guide, it is polite for all to collectively put their money into one envelope, which is then given discreetly to the guide, rather than have each person tipping individually.

SECURITY

On the whole, Vietnam is a relatively safe place. Locals have rarely trusted banks and wealth is buried in the garden, hidden somewhere in the house or kept and worn in the form of gold jewellery. As the country becomes more consumer-oriented there is a greater desire for wealth, and petty thefts appear to be on the increase. As in most countries, it is better not to tempt people so be discreet with your wealth and careful with your possessions.

Most areas are quite safe but persistent beggars, pickpockets and thieves do exist. Some beggars dress as Buddhist monks in the hope of getting money. To avoid being mobbed, it is best not to give anything. What you can do, instead, is to contribute to agencies that are trying to help these people.

Always cultivate an awareness of who is near you, especially in the market place. Do not carry large amounts of cash and do not wear jewellery that can be snatched easily. Teams of pickpockets hang out around the major hotels and bars, and evenings are the most lucrative period for them. Sunglasses perching on the tops of heads, pens in shirt pockets, rings on fingers, and wallets and bags are all targets. When you ride in cyclos or on a motorcycle, make sure that your wallet, camera, handbag or jewellery is tucked away as thieves cruise by on passing motorcycles and grab goods during the day, as well as at night. Foreigners have compounded some of these problems by being too flashy with their wealth. Some have also contributed to a black market in foreign passports by selling their own, and then reporting its loss so as to get a replacement.

When shopping for large items that you cannot fit in your car or carry back with you, try to arrange for the shop to deliver the goods. If this is not possible, hire a cyclo and get on it with your goods, no matter how cramped the space may be, as it is not uncommon for cyclo drivers to make off with your purchases, particularly just prior to Tet.

Like all countries, Vietnam has its seedier side. Many people are poor and foreigners appear to be comparatively wealthy. At night, try to move around in groups if you are walking, travelling by cyclo or using the local transport. Prostitution and the use of drugs are quite widespread. Beware of prostitutes who may be linked to thieves. AIDS (called SIDA in Vietnam) is also present and the authorities are only just starting to monitor the problem. It is illegal to have a Vietnamese girl in a hotel room overnight with you and as everyone going in or out of hotels is being monitored, you can expect trouble if you try this.

Knife attacks or hold-ups are not uncommon either. When accosted, it is better to give up your money than put up a struggle as the past 40 years or so has shown the people how cheap life is, and foreigners are not immune to a swiftly-wielded knife jab.

NIGHT LIFE

Most people create their own fun with dinner parties, video viewings and so on. There is very little in the way of shows or performances. Restaurants, bars, karaoke set-ups and discotheques exist in the bigger towns. Most places shut down early. It can be hard, if not impossible, to get a meal after 9 p.m. in an established restaurant but a nourishing meal from one of the many street sellers is possible at virtually any hour. Currently, there is an 11.30 p.m. curfew on places of entertainment but the extent to which it is enforced varies.

Because there is such a mix of nationalities working within Vietnam, numerous celebrations are held by each community. These are sometimes widely advertised and you may find yourself enjoying St. Patrick's night with the Irish, St Andrew's with the Scottish and Australia Day, besides joining in the religious festivities of Christmas with Christians and Lebaran with the Muslims. Then, of course, there are the Vietnamese national holidays such as Tet.

MAKING VIETNAM HOME

Settling down is an exciting time full of new discoveries. It can also be stressful as you learn your way around and come to terms with a new job, besides searching for accommodation and establishing a new lifestyle. But once you are settled, a whole new world opens up. You are now spared from the time-consuming tasks of hunting for a house and furniture, or overseeing the workers, and have the free time to participate in social activities and make the most of the opportunities in the country.

— Chapter Five —

CULTURE SHOCK

The term "culture shock" sounds like a newly invented, catchy phrase that covers many things—and that is exactly what it is. More and more people are jetting across the world, visiting countries they know virtually nothing about, and "culture shock" describes the wide and varying range of emotions that they feel. It is a combination of the physical and psychological stresses that are experienced when a person moves into a new environment. Sights, smells and tastes are all different. The people are of a different culture and have a different frame of reference. They think differently, have a different sense of humour and priorities that are different from yours. Then, there is the added problem of communication. You may not speak their language, and hence feel further alienated.

It is not necessarily the locality itself which causes the problems, but the additional stresses that occur within a person as he or she tries to adjust to a foreign place. Its duration can be quite lengthy. Foreigners already settled for several years in a country will still come across the odd moment when they experience culture shock. But knowing what to expect and how it may affect you makes the period of adjustment much easier.

Cultural Comparisons

If you want to feel relaxed and comfortable in the country that you are settling in, the differences between the local people and your own way of thinking and doing things must be examined. They are simply cultural differences. There is no right or wrong involved.

As a child, you were taught what was socially correct within your own culture and society. You were brought up to react a certain way. When you move from country to country, and from culture to culture, this social etiquette alters. For instance, within much of the Western world, embarrassment is shown by downcast eyes, a serious face and a look showing that you wish you were elsewhere. Throughout much of Asia, laughter or smiling is a normal reaction to embarrassment. But when Westerners are faced with this, they judge it against their own social conditioning and often deem it unacceptable, or they may take it as an indication of something other than embarrassment.

You may be tempted to say that you are right, or that your way of doing things is better. Try to avoid imposing your opinion on others. In Vietnam, especially, the mix of visitors spans many continents and even throwing a dinner party for other expatriates may cross several cultural boundaries. Greetings are different and socially acceptable conversation varies, as does the manner in which people treat each other.

Recognising Culture Shock

It is not something that is always obvious. Conversations about the emotional stages that a foreigner goes through—trying to cope with life away from home and the problems encountered—are not usually voiced as freely as restaurant recommendations. The mental adjustments that are required increase the stress level in a person and this manifests itself in a variety of ways.

You question your sanity, for instance, when a minor incident upsets you tremendously. Arguments over the smallest of things become common. Things that you normally cope with easily frustrate you. You become annoyed at your own seeming inability to function efficiently and effectively. You blame yourself, feeling that you are the only one suffering such problems. Problems associated with stress—such as ill health, depression, poor sleeping patterns, lethargy, becoming withdrawn or an alteration of normal behaviour patterns—take hold.

Some new arrivals feel as if the only contacts with Vietnamese that they make are with people out to get something from them. A serving lady welcomes you into the shop with a broad smile and a little voice at the back of your head says "She's only smiling because I'm a foreigner and she thinks I will pay much higher prices than a local would". Someone starts a conversation with you as you wait at the airport for friends to arrive and the same little voice says "He's not really being friendly, he just wants someone to practise his English on". These feelings may emerge when you are tired or worried but unfortunately, they can be a recurring thought. Your fears may have some basis at times but most Vietnamese are simply being courteous and curious about you.

Who Suffers from Culture Shock?

Everyone suffers from culture shock. Even the most travel-weary person who has "been there and seen that" experiences it. Every new country has its own culture. Moving to a new place means a readjustment, no matter how many times you have done it before.

If you have lived in a similar place previously, you may not find it so hard to cope initially. China has historically dominated much of Vietnam and many aspects of its culture have been adopted here. So if you are familiar with Chinese ways, you may already know about the Confucian set of social values or the traditional practice of gift-giving during the New Year. But there are also many differences between the two cultures and you may find yourself expecting one thing but getting another.

Unanticipated reactions from another person or a surprise emotion of your own, can cause culture shock. A first-timer usually expects everything to be new and different and realises that he will have to tackle a range of problems in trying to settle down. However, a long-term expatriate who has been through the worry of moving, finding friends and learning a new language, often thinks he has overcome some of the other issues as well. Well, this is usually not the case. One expatriate complained, "I know better and it shouldn't have happened to me!" after an air-conditioner was placed in the wrong position for the third time because she had not been there to supervise the installation personally.

HOW MIGHT IT AFFECT YOU?

The issues and problems facing any foreigner who settles in Vietnam are different, depending on the role he or she is expected to play.

The Business Person

You usually acquire friends through work and soon become very busy. Many businesses require their staff to put in long hours and you may seem to eat, breathe and sleep work. It is challenging and highly rewarding and you are often working with minimal supervision. Most of your time is spent thinking of work and your routine soon revolves around it. The office staff and your business associates become friends.

You are here to work and it takes precedence over everything else. It may be difficult, but necessary, to take time off to socialise with people outside your immediate circle of friends and colleagues. Find time to relax, stay healthy and to maintain a balanced view of life. Most jobs are office-bound and it is difficult to get access to some of the limited sports facilities after office hours. It is easy to over-indulge in food and drink, particularly if you are living in a hotel and eating out for all your meals.

Many of your culture shock issues will concern your dealings with Vietnamese who are your work partners, office staff or clients, or within the government bureaucracy. Instructions at work may not be carried out the way you wanted, or things may not happen when you think they should. Mistakes will be ignored or hidden from you until you find them out for yourself.

The Working Spouse

While you spend most of your time working, family pressures are also building up. You probably do not get much spare time to spend with your spouse or children and they are feeling the need for your presence and support. Evening work functions or social invitations mean that there is little time to sit down and relax together. Whatever little free time you may have will probably be spent reading and organising your personal paper work.

Often, a spouse may seem to become less independent and more demanding of your time, making you feel trapped. It is important for couples to spend time together, relating their individual experiences. This is especially crucial in the early days of settling in. Discuss the amount of free time you have together and agree on a routine. Leave a couple of nights through the week, a lunch hour or Sunday mornings free to be together. Explain the work situation and the work relationships between different people. Most people assume that your spouse understands at least the basics of your work scenario and it may save a social *faux pas* over the dinner table later.

The Non-working Spouse

This is usually, although not always, the wife. It can be a wonderful time to try all sorts of new activities and indulge yourself. But it can also be a very frustrating role as you will probably see little of your partner. The office provides a routine for your spouse. He may not understand your problems or simply does not have the time to help you do much about them. It is usually your job to go house-hunting, do the shopping, recruit domestic staff and train them, and build a group of friends outside the work environment. Social organising is left up to you.

You may feel as if you have lost your own identity. Hearing yourself referred to regularly as "Tony's wife", for instance, does not do a great deal for your ego. But you are associated with your spouse's company, whether you like it or not. You may not always feel free to say what you like and do what you want but, at the same time, you need to find a balance and just be yourself.

Part-time or full-time work is available depending on your skills and experience. Seeking work can be frustrating and time-consuming without your normal contacts. You may have to settle for a less than satisfying career move or a lower pay scale than you were accustomed to. There may also be problems obtaining a work visa.

Parents

You have all the problems of being a spouse and more! Health, security and ensuring that your children have a proper education and upbringing are the greatest additional worries. Specific issues vary depending on the age of the child. However, discipline is a recurring problem. The Vietnamese love children Aside from hiring your own nanny, drivers, waitresses and housekeepers all act as baby-sitters at some point of time. Unfortunately, they are not in a situation to discipline your child. Culturally, tight controls are not placed on Vietnamese children. This creates two problems: the child may be allowed to get into a dangerous situation due to insufficient restraint or, less seriously, they can become spoilt brats as they work out very quickly what they can get away with and who they can order around.

Young children are very much loved by the Vietnamese and you can expect strangers to come up and hug, talk and play games with your child. This can be a blessing as waitresses divert your child's attention, allowing you to eat a meal in relative peace. But it can also become overbearing. Some children hate the feeling of being constantly pestered when they step outside, or being stared at as they sit in a car. If you endorse this friendly behaviour from strange Vietnamese, be prepared to reconcile it with the warnings you may have told your child about never going near strangers at home.

Vietnamese tend to pinch young children as a sign of affection but it can be quite painful for the child and even leave bruises. Older children learn to watch for it and dodge a hand that comes near them but you will have to fend off hands reaching for younger children, unless you decide to put up with the frequent tears it produces.

There are schools and playgroups for youngsters (see the section on children in Chapter 4, Settling Down) but facilities are limited. Most teenagers are in boarding schools elsewhere but come to join their parents during the school holidays. The main problems for them are meeting people their age and finding things to do. Despite these difficulties, there is a wide range of opportunities that may not be so readily available elsewhere. Besides the exposure to a new country and culture and the learning experience that this brings, foreign languages, art classes, lessons in martial arts and all sorts of activities are an option in Vietnam. Most parents agree that, for a child, the advantages that come from living in a foreign country far outweigh the disadvantages.

Singles

Arriving alone can be lonely as there is no instant friend to share experiences and talk things over with. It may seem a little harder to make friends without a spouse who is also meeting new people.

However, there are many others in the same situation who are travelling or have come for work, so it can be quite easy to meet up with them and socialise over outings and dinners.

CALENDAR STAGES OF CULTURE SHOCK

Culture shock affects people in different ways. Over time, its impact on each person changes. Broadly, there are four stages of culture shock and an approximate time span can be allocated to each one. However, depending on your own circumstances and the speed with which you settle down, make friends, develop a happy routine and begin to feel at home, the actual timing of these stages will differ. There is also the culture shock of going home again. After living overseas for a few years or longer, you have changed your ways and it can be difficult to re-acclimatise.

Initially, 0–2 Months

Culture shock starts the second you descend from the clouds and see Vietnam unfolding before you. Coping with the weather, the traffic, where to shop for certain items that are not readily available, where and how to hire domestic staff or drivers and how to steer your way through the bureaucratic jungle of officialdom are all subjects that you will rapidly find yourself discussing with other foreigners.

There is the excitement of exploring a new place, the challenge of new work, shopping for bargains and meeting friendly people. While it is certainly not home, the place is not all that bad and you will be able to cope. "It's not as bad as I thought it might be" is a common early statement. Each day is a new learning experience and something to look forward to. Most people stay in a hotel or take up short-term accommodation while they look for something more permanent. There are certainly disappointments and things that may be hard to come to terms with. Everyone has their own levels of tolerance. For some, it is the rats and cockroaches, the level of poverty, the sight of people relieving themselves in public, the beggars and many amputees from the war, the varying standards of hygiene or the slow pace of work in the office.

The health of most people is far from perfect in the first few weeks and local food may well upset the stomach. An inability to sleep through the night is common. The extra fatigue that this causes makes it simply harder to cope with the new day's problems. The other side of the coin is mental overstimulation. Everything is new: the faces, language, roads, prices and friends. Mental overload occurs as you try to come to terms with what seem to be simple things like remembering the name of someone you met yesterday, and how to get back to your hotel when you are only two blocks away. This happens to everyone and most people will not expect a newcomer to remember their name and are quite happy to repeat it for you. Nobody expects you to be on top of everything in the first few weeks, so allowances are made as you settle in.

The Enthusiasm is Wearing Off, 3–6 Months

By now, the veneer is wearing off and the constant call of the cyclo drivers or the sellers has begun to wear thin. The place no longer appears cheap to live in. The problems of short-term accommodation are becoming painfully obvious and you may be getting frustrated about the difficulties of finding affordable longer-term accommodation. You still have not settled into a satisfactory routine and the lack of exercise and all that restaurant food is beginning to show. The friends you initially met and were happy to go out with are annoying you a little. You realise that they do not replace the soulmates you had at home. You are probably starting to feel homesick.

Whether you are working in a business or are a spouse working at setting up a home in the country, you will begin to feel inefficient and ineffective. Things do not seem to be progressing as fast as you would like and every small thing takes a long time to do. You find yourself struggling with issues that you think you should already have come to terms with. No longer do you have the excuse that you have only just arrived. Where does the time in the day go? Weariness sets in.

For the non-working spouse, you are getting a little bored. At first, it was all right to traipse around town learning about the streets and the shops, chatting with new people and looking for friends. But, increasingly, these things seem meaningless and there is little satisfaction in how you are spending the day. This particularly affects those who were used to working, but had to give up their job to accompany their spouse overseas. Having the whole day to yourself seemed like a luxury at first but has quickly become unrewarding. On top of this, the motivation to get up and do things is often slack and you feel lethargic.

You start blaming many things on the country and the people. You easily get upset and try to resolve this with anger. Things still do not seem right, and it is not just the intellectual issues. You thought the belly had finally adjusted to the food and water but just when you least need it, you have another relapse.

Settling Down, 6–12 Months On

You may have coped with (or ignored) certain matters in the short term but now realise that you cannot live with them on a long-term basis and will have to do something positive about them. So you set out to tackle the issue and feel better for it. Now, you are really settling in. Work has taken on a routine. The house is becoming settled and household staff know your preferences. The language is much more familiar and you begin to experiment with it in the market place as you buy. The driver knows the places you visit regularly and the central shops and streets are becoming familiar. You still feel a little inefficient but you are doing quite well. The bad days get fewer and fewer as you get busier.

Long-term—One Year and Beyond

You are happy and settled, involved in the issues of living that would face you anywhere in the world. You have plenty of friends and lead a busy but enjoyable life. Work is familiar and progresses smoothly. The initial problems you faced when you arrived seem to have become a blur and are now fondly joked about. You take newcomers under your wing and can give plenty of advice on how to handle the day-to-day problems. Things that threw you off-track when you first arrived are now scarcely noticed, and trips overseas can even be a little inconvenient as they interfere with your busy schedule.

Life still has its highs and lows. The unexpected home disaster or staffing issue will still occur but you bounce back from these with the help of friends. It is usually the small things. For instance, your cook knows that she should wash a can of kidney beans free of its juices and does the same to the can of baked beans you rarely buy! Generally, you feel very comfortable with the Vietnamese culture and sense that you have adjusted well. At times, though, you are thrown off balance, realising that you have only a superficial understanding of the Vietnamese way of life. It takes years and an excellent command of the language to really understand the people.

GOING HOME—REVERSE CULTURE SHOCK

At some stage, most foreigners will plan to return home. If you have been making regular trips home, you may not feel that the final move back will be too much of an issue. But short-term breaks that are spent catching up with family and friends are not the same as the final move back. Home seems a very familiar place and you think you will be comfortable there immediately. Again, because you do not expect to experience difficulty adjusting back to a well-known place, you find that you are unprepared to cope when problems do arise, and so suffer culture shock in reverse.

Life at home may seem to have changed little while you have been away, but you have changed. On your return, people will be curious about where you have been and how you lived, but this is usually only a temporary curiosity. Unless they are also well travelled, most people find it hard to relate to your experiences and do not want to listen to a three-hour account of where you have been or of the politics or business opportunities in Vietnam. Their eyes quickly glaze over or they move away politely. You may feel as if you are being forced to forget those years overseas. Keeping in touch with close friends you had throughout this period will help.

Similarly, household knick-knacks that you picked up along the way may look completely out of place back in your own country. Children like to wear the "in things" and what they wore in Vietnam may be socially unacceptable to their friends at home.

While changes at home may appear minimal, you will still find that your friends' children have grown up, weddings and celebrations have occurred which you could not attend and you are out of step with all the news, gossip and happenings in your home town. Social conversations often revolve around these and you will feel a little left out. Work on catching up on those things that are important to you. It may be the latest music releases, movies, books, gossip or politics.

Worse still, after settling back into your home routine, beware of boredom. In the work place in Vietnam, you probably had less direct supervision and back home, the work can seem less inspiring. Also, you will find that you cannot go over to neighbouring Thailand for a few days' relaxation. Shopping does not take forever and there are no antique shops to explore. Of course there are great libraries, sports facilities and all sorts of things that you may not have had easy access to in Vietnam. It is simply a time of readjusting again.

HOW TO COPE WITH CULTURE SHOCK

You cannot avoid culture shock but you can minimise it. There are no instant solutions but the most important thing is to recognise culture shock for what it is. You will experience good days and bad ones so learn not to put the blame on someone or something else.

Learn about Your New Home

Start preparing yourself before you move. Learn what you can in advance from a library, Vietnamese migrants who may live in your area or from somebody who has visited the country. Ask them for their impressions. Some information may be out of date but you can, at least, start to build a picture of the place and begin to know what to expect when you arrive. Contact staff who are already in Vietnam and hear what they have to say and what they recommend that you bring along.

Some companies allow you to make an advance visit to the area in Vietnam where you will be stationed. See what is available with respect to housing, schooling, shopping and what the costs are. If you are lucky, you will be able to use this information to finalise negotiations with your company about the away-from-home allowances. Other companies send the employed spouse out there immediately while the other partner stays behind to pack up, plan the shipment, take the children out of school and move to Vietnam a little later. While it may be less than desirable to be apart for a few months, it does allow you to share valuable information with your spouse about the specific conditions. Some careful planning at this stage can make things easier for both of you in the long run.

On arriving, ask questions. The Vietnamese are very friendly and willing to explain things or help you, as are most expatriates. If you have a problem, ask someone about it. Simply understanding why something has occurred is half the battle won. You will not feel so bad about what has happened and will find it much easier to avoid the same thing in future.

Make a Comfortable Home

It does not matter if you are staying in a hotel room or a rented house or apartment. Turn this place into your own sanctuary as quickly as possible. Make it suit you and your lifestyle. Before arriving in Vietnam, think hard about what you will bring and what is to remain in storage. If you are going to be in the country for any length of time, make your place into a home. Bring some personal items. Photos.

pictures and ornaments are some of the best items for making a strange room yours. Any of the good international moving companies should be able to help you plan what to take and advise on what will travel well. Many have booklets listing all the things to consider in the countdown to moving.

Talk and Laugh

One of the best ways of relieving stress is to talk about it and laugh it off with friends as you each share the problems you have had. Your stories may not seem as bad when you talk to someone else. Through this process, you will discover that you are not the only one experiencing such problems. It will also help provide solutions to all those nagging doubts that have been building up inside you and which are starting to get you down—problems such as dealing with servants or someone at work, where to buy something, and so on.

Many people keep these problems to themselves, feeling unable to confide in others, but sharing the experiences with a spouse or friend can help. Write them down if you prefer, in letters home or a diary that you can look back on later. You will then be able to see how well you have made the transition to your new home.

Keep Busy and Find Friends

As in most places, foreigners who have already settled in are generally very welcoming towards new arrivals. It is up to you to fit in. The local people are also friendly and many speak English, so it is easy to make friends when you first arrive. Finding friends is one of the keys to settling down in any new country. It is not easy and there will be many people who are pleasant company but will never be true friends. Persevere—it is worthwhile.

One friend is not enough. Vietnam has a very transient foreign population and people can move on unexpectedly. Join various social activities so you can meet new people. Enlarge the circle of people you know. Talk with those who have a positive attitude towards living in Vietnam and you will find that it rubs off on you too. Socialise outside your work environment. Everyone works enough without having to talk about it through every dinner party as well. Meeting people from other fields of work has the additional advantage of injecting new ideas or information.

This may mean getting involved in things that you would not normally bother with, such as church groups, running clubs, tennis, golf, bridge or language classes, but these are ways in which you can meet more people. In time, you will find somebody with a personality and a sense of humour that appeals to you. You may not find your kindred spirit but you may meet a fellow traveller, photographer, shopper, bridge player or food lover. Ask people you meet what they do besides work and you will soon find out the range of established clubs, meetings, games and sports that are available in your area. Being able to have an honest talk and a good laugh with a friend goes a long way towards overcoming culture shock.

Foreigners from the same cultural background often group together. It is relaxing and allows them to chat in their own language and share news and gossip from home. These groups are a source of instant friends who have had to go through a similar culture-shock experience as yours. However, it is easy to rely on them excessively so that you avoid having to cope with the "real" world outside. Such a move will not help you adjust to your new home and, over time, will only exacerbate the feelings of loneliness and alienation.

Do Not Always Complain

It is easy to blame all the difficulties you are experiencing on the new country, its culture and people. But many of these problems are common in other countries across the world, even though they may take slightly different forms for different reasons. You may encounter problems such as power blackouts, traffic jams that prevent you from arriving at a meeting on time or tradesmen who do not show up as promised to fix things in your house. The weather is hot and humid in many parts of the tropics and air-conditioners can break down wherever you are! Sure, such things are frustrating, but it is not fair to imply that they occur only in Vietnam.

Set Your Own Goals and Work Towards Them
You may have altered your lifestyle greatly. Spouses may have had to forfeit their career or put it on hold. Business people may no longer have easy access to their outside work activities such as clubs or sports. Substitute these with new goals. Learn the language or a new sport or game, advance your photographic skills or plan to lose weight. Develop yourself and do not feel as if it is wasted time, or time put on hold. Make the most of being somewhere different.

Take a Mental Break
When it all gets too much and you are mentally exhausted, get away. This may mean a few days at the beach or, if you are lucky, going overseas. A mental break is what is essential and this can be possible without having to travel. Take all of Sunday off and retreat into a good book, eat and drink (without discussing business) at the best restaurant in town, enjoy a massage or go to bed early and disconnect the phone. The solution will depend on how much time you can spare. But do not struggle on and pretend that you cannot take even an evening off. Mentally, you need it and you will also work better, with renewed enthusiasm, when your mind is sufficiently rested.

Separate the Problems
For those who have no other significant problems to deal with, moving to another country is not all that difficult. But if other problems already exist—particularly a difficult work situation, promotion to a new job you are not familiar with, marital problems, teenagers or children going through difficult stages, a new baby, a family separation or family problems at home—the issues of culture shock can get tangled up with these, making it a much worse situation

for you to cope with emotionally. Try to separate them in your mind and do not blame the country for home problems or, alternatively, blame a family member for culture shock issues.

Stay Healthy

Watch out for certain foods. Most people are well aware of avoiding ice and uncooked foods when they first arrive in a country. The stomach takes time to settle and get used to new bugs. There are also other foods worth avoiding, at least initially, while you come to terms with the country, as they may cause you sleepless nights or ill health.

Monosodium glutamate (MSG) is widely used in cooking here. It goes under a variety of trade names such as Vedan or Aji-no-moto. Widely used in Asian countries as a flavour enhancer, it resembles very shiny salt crystals. Unfortunately, some people suffer anything from mild to violent allergic reactions to it. Common minor reactions that tend to set in after a few hours are: a dryness of the throat, rapid heartbeats similar to an anxiety attack, headaches, sleepless nights and, if asleep, weird dreams that cause you to wake up suddenly. Most restaurants use MSG, but some in much greater quantities than others. If you begin to suffer any of these reactions, watch to see if it always happens after eating at a certain place, and check if your dinner companions suffered similarly. If so, strike the restaurant off your list Many maids cook with MSG as well, so check your own kitchen if you are susceptible to it. The local coffee is strong so if you are having problems, it is a good idea to avoid it. Try the tea instead. Some restaurants sell cups of imported instant coffee, such as Nescafe.

Life can be a social whirl. Lunches and dinners seem to blur into one. On top of a busy work schedule, there is plenty of entertaining to do and social functions to attend. Going out every night for dinner, meeting new people and having a few drinks can seem fun and certainly keeps you from feeling bored or lonely, particularly if you live on your own in a hotel. But it can take its toll physically. The mental stress of working or living in a new place, combined with late nights and lots of food and drink, quickly exhausts you and will not leave you feeling fresh and able to cope with a new day. Have a couple of early nights through the week to recuperate. Avoid alcohol and make sure you get enough sleep.

Take It Easy

Make life easy on yourself as much as possible. There are enough difficulties in everyday living without adding more. Employ a house-keeper or driver who speaks English. This may cost a little more initially but you will get settled much faster and, as Vietnamese is not an easy language to master quickly, the expense is worth it.

Help your memory as it is being bombarded with all these new sights and faces. Get name cards from people, businesses and shops as you go. People do not mind writing out their name for you or handing you a business card, and it often saves future embarrassment. Not only are you more likely to be able to put a name, face and business association together correctly but you have a greater chance of spelling and pronouncing names properly too. Street names can sound very similar and before you familiarise yourself with the roads, it can be hard to remember exactly where you have been. By asking for a business card, you can return to the place with ease. It also allows you to pass on a recommendation of a good shop or restaurant with confidence. Card printing is quick and cheap, so have a box done for yourself so that you, too, can give them to people with whom you would like to maintain contact.

Learn to Enjoy Vietnam

A little extra effort is required initially to ensure that you and your family are happy living in Vietnam (read Chapter 4, Settling Down for further hints). Be determined to make a go of it. Some people rotate their schedule, spending a few weeks in Vietnam and a few weeks back home. This does not allow you to really develop friendships and you will not be properly settled in either place. If your work demands it, fair enough. But if you are a non-working spouse, resist the temptation unless you are forced to share your time between a husband or wife in Vietnam and children in boarding school elsewhere. If you are in Vietnam for an indefinite period, depending on the outcome of business ventures, do not fall into the trap of not making an effort to find friends and build up a social life just because there is a chance that you may have to leave soon. It is better to become involved and feel sorry that you have to leave earlier than anticipated than not to have made the effort and spend several years in Vietnam feeling bored, wishing you were leaving soon.

Learn to love your time in Vietnam. Treat it as a new opportunity and the time will fly by all too quickly.

Something new you may want to try: street barbers are a common sight throughout the country.

Chapter Six

COMMUNICATION

Learning the Vietnamese language is a frustrating and time-consuming task. It is also fulfilling, helps break down barriers between people and is the only way that you will start to really understand the Vietnamese. You will make endless mistakes as you grapple with part Vietnamese, part English, but will soon learn to see the funny side of it. For instance, a woman wanted her driver to return from lunch at 1 p.m. and take her to an outer suburb of Ho Chi Minh City called Thu Duc. After saying this in a lengthy sentence in English, and upon seeing the look of non-comprehension on the driver's face, she simplified it to what she thought was the essence of the message:

"One o'clock, Thu Duc," pointing at herself as she spoke. The driver nodded and returned at one o'clock with two live ducks in the car!

Problems like this are frequent. There will be many occasions when you think you are saying a Vietnamese word correctly, yet no one understands your accent, or the tone that you used was wrong. New visitors get exasperated trying to tell a cyclo or taxi driver the name of a street. A crowd gathers around trying to understand what the foreigner is saying, and his voice gets louder and louder, until someone pulls out a piece of paper and a pen. When he has written his destination down, a look of understanding dawns, everyone smiles, and both driver and visitor head off in the right direction. So do not hesitate to write street names down. It can save you a lot of time!

That does not imply that it is not worth trying to master the spoken language. You will find no shortage of teachers and even a little help goes a long way. The local people appreciate the fact that you are trying to speak their language. Mistakes are accepted good-naturedly and several people will usually stop to give you an impromptu lesson.

Cross-cultural friendship that transcends language barriers—an expatriate and his Vietnamese friend enjoying a night out.

THE LANGUAGE

The Vietnamese language is spoken throughout the country, although some of the ethnic minorities do not speak it widely. There are slight differences between the north and the south with regard to certain words and pronunciations, and people from Hue speak with an accent that is difficult to understand. The differences are usually not of such magnitude as to make communication a problem. For instance, the national dress, the *ao dai,* is pronounced "ao yai" by a southerner, but "ao zai" by a northerner. Northeners tend to have a slightly clipped accent and have a tendency to switch the "l" and "n" sounds around in Vietnamese words. If you speak Vietnamese, it just means that it is easy to tell which part of the country a Vietnamese comes from.

History of the Language

Linguistic authorities still argue over the origin of the Vietnamese language. It is derived from a mixture of the Thai, Mon-Khmer and Muong languages and, since then, the majority of its words have come from Chinese. By the 9th century, the written Chinese language of Chu Nho was used throughout much of eastern Asia for written communication, but the characters were pronounced differently throughout the regions. Spoken Vietnamese was quite distinct from Chu Nho and from the languages spoken in other areas. While Chu Nho was used for official documents, it was adapted by 13th century Vietnamese scholars into their own script called Chu Nom, which found its way into unofficial documents and literary works.

In the 16th century, Catholic missionaries arriving from Spain, Portugal, Italy and France wanted to be able to communicate more easily to spread their message. Under the guidance of Father Alexander-de-Rhodes, a romanised system of writing called Quoc Ngu was developed. This enabled spoken Vietnamese to be written in a romanised alphabet. In 1651, the first Vietnamese-Portuguese-Latin dictionary using this script was published. Since 1920, this version has been the official language. Foreign words have been added, mostly during times of French and American influence when new things were brought into the country. From the French came *dau petit pois* for peas and *ca rot* for carrots. Coffee is *ca phe*. The Americans can be thanked for *mac ga rin* for margarine and *quan jeans* for jeans.

ANGLICISED VIETNAMESE

An anglicised version of the Vietnamese language can sometimes be seen in books. For instance, there is no "f" in the language, yet the tallest mountain in Vietnam, Phan Si Pan, can be seen written as "Fansipan". Not only has "f" replaced the "ph", but the individual syllables have been combined to make one word. Most Vietnamese words are monosyllabic but compound, and several words are needed to convey the meaning. The Vietnamese spelling of their country is "Viet Nam" but the anglicised version, and the one used in this book, is "Vietnam". Longer words consisting of more than one syllable now exist within the language, but they are usually new words, such as *yaourt* (yoghurt).

TONES

Vietnamese is a tonal language and the meaning of the word alters depending on the inflection used when it is spoken. In the north, there are six tones, but in the south, only five are used. Southerners make little distinction between the third and fourth tones listed below. For instance, the word *ma* means a ghost, *má* means mother, *mà* stands for that or which, *mả* is tomb, *mã* means horse and *mạ* is rice seedling.

To differentiate between the words, five different accents are used to indicate the way the word should be spoken. The sixth tone is recognised by the absence of any marks. The tones are :

- A rising tone, in a high pitch, indicated by an acute accent (a line above the letter rising from left to right) as in á.
- A falling tone, indicated by a grave (a line above the letter falling from left to right) as in à.
- A low, rising tone which starts low, falls slightly, then rises as in

å. This sound is similar to the tone put on a questioning word in English.

- A high, broken tone where the voice starts just above the normal range and dips a little, then rises very rapidly. This is marked by a tilde as in ã.
- A low, broken tone where a dot is placed under the word as in ạ, and the word is said in a low tone which falls and ends abruptly.
- An even tone has no markings and is said in the middle range of the voice.

This takes quite a lot of practice and a learner will often find it easier to read and write Vietnamese than to say it in a way that is clearly understood. A common mistake is to end a question on a rising tone, as is the custom in English. This causes confusion in Vietnamese and, instead of indicating a question, the use of a rising tone alters the meaning of the last word.

THE ALPHABET

Because of its phonetic nature, the alphabet used is not the same as in English.

There are 12 vowel symbols which make 11 varieties of sound:

a   as in father.
ă   as in mum.
â   as in but, cut.
e   as in cat.
ê   as in hay.
i or y as in fee, tea or me.
o   as in floor.
ô   as in no or oh. This is the sound used in Ho Chi Minh City.
ơ   as in fur.
u   as in foot or a long, drawn-out oooh sound, like clue.
ư   has no real equivalent in English and is similar to a short "ergh".

Twenty-eight consonant symbols are used to make 21 sounds. Many have the same sound as in English but there are some exceptions.

b or p	as in bed, borrow.
c, k and q	a hard "c" or "k", as in can, king, quick.
ch	at the beginning of a word it sounds like chariot but at the end of a word, it is much harder, sounding almost like the "k" in lick.
đ	note the bar across the "d", as in dog.
d, dz or gi	in the north, pronounced softly as a "ge" sound as in change and in the south, with a "y" sound as in yacht. Northern people may write "d" as "dz" to help foreigners pronounce the letter correctly. The letter "z" is not traditionally in the language, however.
g or gh	as in go.
h	as in hat.
kh	as in the German Bach.
l	as in love, label.
m	as in me, method.
n	as in not, narrow.
ng or ngh	as in singer or sung, and slightly aspirated.
nh	at the beginning of a word, like the "ny" sound in the Spanish *mañana* or in canyon. At the end of a word, it sounds similar to "ng" as in fighting.
ph	sounds like "f", as in phone or funny.
r	in the south, rolled but otherwise used as in run; in the north, softened to a "z" sound as in zone.
s	in the south, is softened to a "sh" sound like show; in the north, stays as "s" as in sunny.
t	as in tomorrow.
th	similar to English but much more air is let out on the "h" sound, as in thin, method or breath.
tr	in the south, shorter than in English usage, as in entry; in the north, sounds more like a "ch" sound, so the word

"trance" would be pronounced "chance".

v   as in very, although, in the south, it can sound a little more like the "z" sound in zone.

x   in the south, like an "s" sound in see; in the north, a little softer like the "sh" in shell.

GRAMMAR RULES

Here, the language is relatively simple. Words are not altered to indicate plurals or gender. For instance, a greeting for a single woman is *chào chị* and, for a number of women standing in a group, *chào các chị,* so the addition of *các* indicates the plural form. Words are not changed to indicate tense either. Instead, another classifier or tool word must be added to the sentence to make the meaning clear. *Đang* indicates continuous tense, *đã* past tense and *sẽ* is used for the future tense. For instance:

I am going to the market.   *Tôi đang đi chởi.*
I have gone to the market.   *Tôi đã đi chởi.*
I will go to the market.   *Tôi sẽ đi chởi*

Modifiers follow, so the noun is followed by the adjective and the verb is followed by the adverb. Instead of saying "red car", the people say "car red". All non-essential words are omitted and even the subject can be left out where it is obvious.

Descriptors are used before a noun to indicate the type of noun it is. For instance, *trái* means "a piece of" and is used before the noun for fruit. *Con* indicates an animal or certain things, for example, *Con cá này bao nhiêu?* means "How much is the fish?" *Cái* is used for wooden items and some other articles such as a table, which translates into *cái bàn*. There are no strict rules applying to *con* and *cái* and the words are often substituted with *quả* in the north. The correct usage of each has to be memorised.

NAMES

Given names always come after the family name. For instance, in

Nguyen Ngoc Lam, Nguyen is the family name and Ngoc Lam are the given names and the person will be called Lam, although this will be modified with the correct form of address.

You will find that certain names are very common. Nguyen is the most widespread family name used by about 50% of the population, as the Nguyen emperors allowed people to take on their family name. Other common names are Le, Phan, Tran, Ngo, Do, Dao, Duong, Dang, Dinh and Hoang.

Traditionally, the middle name was either Thị to indicate a girl, or Văn to indicate a boy, but this is no longer strictly followed and these qualifiers may be replaced with a second name. Children are given a first name with a special meaning as parents believe that the lives of their children may be affected by the chosen name. Hence, a beautiful name may ensure a better life for the child. Males may be named after the season they were born in, such as Xuan (Spring) or Thu (Autumn), or after qualities that the parent hopes the child will have, like Minh (bright), Phuc (luck) or Duc (virtuous). Examples of female names are Hong (rose), Lien (lotus), Huong (perfume) or Trinh (virginal girl).

Children may also be named by order of birth. In the north, the first born is named Ca (meaning big or biggest) and the second, Hai (number two). To make matters more confusing, in the south the first born is called Hai (number two) and the second child, Ba (number three) and so on. No child is called Mot (number one). Ut means smallest and is a name used for the youngest child. Another tradition is to name the child after the zodiac sign of the lunar year in which they were born. The Vietnamese work on a lunar calendar which is very similar to the Chinese one. Time is not divided into centuries but into *hoi*, which are blocks of 60 years. Each *hoi* is subdivided into *can*, 10-year periods, and also *ky*, 12-year periods. Each of these 12 years has a zodiac significance and is named after an animal, and so a child may be know as Suu (Buffalo) or Ty (Snake), indicating the year in which he or she was born.

Nicknames

Families often have nicknames for members. At home, children have ugly nicknames such as Bo (cow), Tho (rabbit), or Gau (bear) so that evil spirits are not attracted to the child No matter what a person's given name is, a sister from the south will always call her eldest brother "Brother Hai" as a mark of respect and each family member will be referred to by their position in the family. Northerners do not follow this custom and will call their family by their given names.

For business purposes, some Vietnamese take on a Western name as most foreigners cannot pronounce their Vietnamese name correctly. Christian Vietnamese will take on a baptismal name. Monks and nuns are given new names too. Parents may also be called by their oldest child's name. This is a sign of respect to the mother and father as they are no longer considered children themselves, but are old and responsible enough to have their own child.

Married Women

Prior to 1975, a married woman would take on the title of "Mrs." and change from her maiden name to her husband's family name, as is the custom in the West. Now, she does not change her family name and there is no distinction between "Mrs." and "Miss". But if people have known her husband before meeting her, they may call her by her husband's first name. This practice is carried over to foreigners so do not be surprised or offended if people call you "Mrs. Tony" and continue to do so even after they know you well. Vietnamese children take their father's family name.

FORMS OF ADDRESS AND GREETING

How you address a person is considered important and shows the level of respect and friendship between the two parties. Vietnamese culture accords people different status levels and how they are addressed reflects this. If you are doubtful over how you should address a person, it is better to adopt a more formal form of address rather than an informal one. Always treat older people or those in higher positions of authority with respect and deference, and greet them before the others in a group.

According to folklore, all Vietnamese are related to each other and this belief is reinforced by their language. Every form of address is based on a family relationship, such as an uncle, aunt or little sister. Chao means "hello" and the common greetings are listed below.

Common Greetings

chào ông	to an older or important man (grandfather).
chào anh	to a younger man (brother, husband).
chào chú	to a man younger than your father but older than you (uncle).
chào bà	to an old or important woman (grandmother).
chào chị	to an older woman (sister).
chào cô	to a younger woman (aunt).
chào em	to a child, male or female; someone subordinate to you; or someone close, such as a husband or very good friend.
chào bạn	to a friend of your age.

A more formal greeting will include the person's name. For instance if you meet Nguyen Ngoc Lam at a business meeting, you would say "*Chào anh* Lam" or "*Chào anh* Ngoc Lam". To be even more formal, you would say "*Chào* Nguyen Ngoc Lam". The male descriptor "*anh*" is the equivalent of our "Mr." and is usually included in a greeting as a sign of respect, unless the whole name is used.

Even in a relatively informal situation in which friends greet each other, you will hear "*Chào anh* Lam" although, among younger people, "*Chào* Lam" is becoming more common. If you greet a woman, no distinction is made over whether she is married or not. The choice of descriptor depends on her age and your age relative to hers. Among the older generation, an official's name is preceded with *đồng chí,* meaning "comrade" and monks or nuns are usually addressed as *thầy,* or a priest as *cha* and a nun as *xỗ.* Professional people may be called by their title, for instance "Mr. Director" or "Mrs. Vice-Director".

A typical interaction would be as follows: *Chào cô* ("hello" to a younger lady), *Có khỏe không?* (literally "Are you healthy?", the equivalent of the English "How are you?"). The reply will be *Khỏe, cám ổn* (literally, "Healthy, thank you" and a substitute for the Western "Fine, thanks"). Alternatively, you may say *Chị khỏe chứ,* which also means "How are you?" but requires no answer. If someone asks you "How you are?", it is impolite to say you are sick and launch into a description about your illness. Avoid this and just give the standard reply.

HOW TO BE INTRODUCED

You can introduce yourself to someone but it is more correct to find a third party who knows both of you to do the task. This is often done in business circles, where who you know is very important and the status of the introducer gives you added credibility. Unfortunately, as the Vietnamese prefer not to introduce themselves, you may get someone telling you that you had a visitor while you were out, but he is unable to tell you who it was. The Vietnamese visitor rarely introduces himself and secretaries or maids may not ask unless you insist that it is part of their work responsibilities to do so.

Traditionally, the Vietnamese do not shake hands but clasp their hands together above waist level and bow slightly as a sign of acknowledgement. It is still used in pagodas or by older people but business greetings are often done in the Western way now. A formal handshake between men may be exchanged, with a nod and slight bow of the head. If the person is a figure of authority, a high official or someone who deserves respect, two hands are used together when shaking hands or exchanging name cards. The Vietnamese do not touch people of the opposite sex so men and women do not shake hands and will nod and smile to each other instead. A handshake may be seen where the Vietnamese woman is quite Westernised and accepts it as a Western practice, or where a Vietnamese businessman realises that it is acceptable to the Western woman.

As in most other aspects, the north tends to be more formal than the south with regard to greetings. For more information, see the gestures and body contact section in Chapter 7, Socialising in Vietnam. If you are greeting people in a group, whether in a family home or business meeting, make sure that you greet each person, including young children. All actions are communicated gently. It is not appropriate to throw your hand into someone else's and pump it vigorously! Even the action of serving you a cup of tea will be done very carefully so that the cup does not clatter onto the tabletop.

FAREWELLS

A handshake or the traditional slight bow with hands together is appropriate when you take leave of someone. It is also polite to say something such as "Best regards to your family" or "Good luck to you" as a parting shot.

USEFUL WORDS

General

Thank you	*Cám ơn.* The other person may reply *Không có chi* (You are welcome)
Hello	*Xin chào*
Goodbye	*Tạm biệt*
Excuse me	*Tôi xin lỗi*
I am very pleased to meet you	*Tôi rất hân hạnh dược gặp anh*
Yes	*Phải*
No	*Không*
What is this?	*Đây là cái gì* (for an object)
Who is this?	*Đây là ai?*
I don't know	*Tôi không biết*

I don't understand.	*Tôi không hiểu*
Maybe	*Có thể*
That's okay/no problem	*Không sao*
Please	*Vui lòng*
Already	*Xong rồi*
Where is the bathroom?	*Câù tiều ổ đâu?*
Go	*Đi đi* (used to brush off beggars or people bothering you)

Numbers

zero	*không*
one	*một*
two	*hai*
three	*ba*
four	*bốn*
five	*năm*
six	*saú*
seven	*bảy*
eight	*tám*
nine	*chín*
ten	*mười*
eleven	*mười một*
twenty	*hai mười*
twenty-one	*hai mười mốt*
one hundred	*một trăm*
one thousand	*một ngàin* (or *ngàn* in the south)
ten thousand	*mười nghìn*
one hundred thousand	*trăm nghìn*
one million	*một triệu*

Days/Time/Calendar

morning	*buôỉ sáng*
lunchtime 11–2	*buôỉ trưa*

afternoon 2–7 p.m.	*buổi chiều*
evening 7–9 p.m.	*buổi tối*
late at night	*ban đêm*
yesterday	*hôm qua*
today	*hôm nay*
tomorrow	*ngày mai*
early	*sớm*
late	*trễ*
Monday	*Thứ Hai*
Tuesday	*Thứ Ba*
Wednesday	*Thứ Tử*
Thursday	*Thứ Năm*
Friday	*Thứ Sáu*
Saturday	*Thứ Bảy*
Sunday	*Chủ Nhật*
month	*tháng*
May	*tháng năm*, the fifth month. Each month is indicated by the word "month" followed by the qualifier, a number indicating which month you are referring to with the exception of January, which is called *Tháng giêng*

Transport

bus station	*bến xe*
taxi	*xe tắc xi*
cyclo	*xe xích lô*
train	*xe lửa*
where is ....?	*ở đâu ....?*
motorbike taxi	*hon đa ôm*
turn right	*quẹo phải*
turn left	*quẹo trái*
stop	*đủng lại*

straight ahead	*thẳng*
wait	*đợi*

Shopping

market	*chợ*
money	*tiền*
post office	*nhà bửu điện*
very expensive	*mắc quá* (colloquial) or *đắt quá*
reduce	*bớt đi*
how much?	*bao nhiêu?*
How much is one kilogram?	*Bao nhiêu một ký?*
cheap	*rẻ quá*
bank	*nhà băng* or *ngân hàng*
shop	*của hàng*
souvenir shop	*của hàng lửu niệm*
book shop	*của hàng sách*

Office/Residence

at work	*nồi làm việc*
office	*văn phòng*
I live here	*Tôi sống ở đây*
My house is located on the street Le Thanh Ton	*Nhà tôi ở trên đường Le Thanh Ton*
41/2	*bốn mươi mốt trên hai*

Emergency

doctor	*bác sĩ*
hospital	*bệnh viện*
pharmacy	*nhà thuộc*
dentist	*nha sĩ*
telephone	*điện thoại*
help	*cứu tôi với*
police	*công an*

Eating

bread	*bánh mì*
vegetables	*rau cải*
rice	*cồm*
lemon	*chanh*
chilli	*ổt*
no sugar	*không đửồng*
ice	*đá*
milk	*sửa*
banana	*chuôí*
meat	*thịt*
beef	*thịt bò*
pork	*thịt heo*
chicken	*gà*
duck	*vịt*
shrimp	*tôm*
fish	*cá*
bring the bill, please	*xin làm ổn, tính tiền*

NON-VERBAL LANGUAGE

The type of non-verbal language most commonly used by new arrivals is the form of communication used when neither party speaks the other's language. It is amazing how much business can be conducted in the market, restaurant, shop or house using sign language. Here, there may be no alternative and both parties are willing as they both want something out of the transaction.

Non-verbal language is also used by all of us when we are communicating, either directly or through a translator, and is often a more accurate indicator of someone's emotions than the actual words said. In a business meeting, you may recognise nervous habits in a colleague which lead you to guess, for instance, that he may be uncertain where he stands in current negotiations, or that the issue being discussed is very important to him. However, not all non-verbal language carries the same meaning in different cultures and you need to be careful about the assumptions made from your observations.

The Vietnamese are very sensitive in relating to people's body language. Regardless of the words you are speaking, they may take offence at your posture, reading something into it. Westerners use tones to help project the emotion and nuances behind the words they are using. The Vietnamese, however, use tones to create different words and hence rely on other factors to convey their emotions. Facial changes are one of the most obvious and commonly used techniques. The fastest way to know that something has gone wrong here is when a person's face goes blank. His countenance is wooden and this indicates that he is deliberately hiding his emotions. Otherwise, his expressions are reasonably animated and quite easy to read.

Signs of Agreement

Nodding of the head by a listener as you talk does not mean that he agrees with what you are saying, only that he can hear you and understand the words.

Eye Contact

Direct eye contact is avoided between strangers, especially when girls and young women meet someone for the first time. It may take time to build up a working relationship with a new staff member and if you are a male, a foreigner and in a position of authority, do not be surprised if eye contact is avoided for an initial period. The person is simply being polite.

However, people will stare at you on the street as you are an object of interest. It is actually impolite to do so and if you stare back, they will usually avert their eyes. In the country areas, people will look at you curiously and smile but in cities such as Ho Chi Minh City, the stares can be more intimidating and less friendly. Just as you may look curiously at a person from one of the hill tribes, remember that you are a foreigner and have different clothes and mannerisms. Not all

Vietnamese will be familiar with these things so you can expect to be studied!

As people speak, they will also cover their mouth with their hand or whatever happens to be handy. This is not a sign of nervousness or a fear of bad breath but a cultural tradition, displayed particularly towards strangers.

Gestures

Pointing at someone with a finger, or pointing the sole of your foot at someone when crossing your legs, is considered rude. The latter is an indication that you think the other person is below you so if you do cross your legs, point your toes downwards. Also impolite is the usual Western gesture of asking someone to come to you, conveyed by turning the palm of the hand upwards, and using the index finger to beckon. In Vietnam, this sign is used only for animals. The people gesture to each other with the palm downwards, and wiggling all four fingers in unison.

Aggressive body stances such as crossing your arms or placing your hands on your hips are also not acceptable. However, if you do such actions as a subconscious aid to thinking, the Vietnamese will relate them to your facial features and accept them as such.

Body Contact

The head has special significance as it is believed that a person's spirit lives there, so never touch someone's head, particularly at the front portion. A different genie resides on the shoulder, so do not put your hand there either. If you do so accidentally, superstitious people believe that you should also touch the other shoulder to offset the bad luck. Also, avoid slapping a friend on the back after a joke.

It is impolite to touch anyone of the opposite sex. Some Western-ised youngsters in the cities may flout social conventions but the Vietnamese are largely a conservative people and in traditional society, even a husband and wife will not hold hands while walking down a street. The only exception is when a foreign woman shakes hands with a Vietnamese man or, perhaps, touches his arm lightly to indicate intensity of feeling without any sexual connotations. However, do not be surprised if a member of the same sex grabs your hand to guide you across the street or places his or her hand on your arm and leaves it there while talking to you. Physical contact between members of the same sex is simply a display of friendship and it is common to see two men or women walking down the road holding hands. This may feel like an invasion of your personal space. Try hard to accept it for the goodwill that it conveys and do not withdraw as this can cause the other person to lose face.

While you will see men holding hands or women touching each other, they do not greet each other in a showy manner. Long-lost friends or family members will not hug each other in a public reunion. Instead, you may see them touch each other on the arm. Similarly, it is not usual to kiss a Vietnamese on each cheek, the way the Westerners do as a form of greeting. If you attempt it, they will probably not pull away and cause you to lose face, but will freeze. They become very self-conscious and the conversation that follows may be very awkward for both parties.

CONVERSATION

There are many subtle nuances and allusions in speech and gesture. Some of these do not translate well but as you learn the language, you begin to realise how complex it is to fully comprehend all facets of a conversation. The Vietnamese can be disarmingly direct in some matters. They may tell you that you are five minutes late to work in the morning. It is quite polite to quiz someone about their age, religion and, of course, family life, and for someone to ask you how much you earn or how much you have spent on something just purchased. The Vietnamese are very curious, eager to learn and anxious to figure out where you may fit in terms of status, so such questions are common. You can choose to be evasive in answering some of them and learn a few "throw away" lines that indicate politely that you do not want to answer. For instance, when you are asked how much something costs, or how much rent you are paying for your house, you can simply laugh and say "too much".

While the people can be direct in this way, they can be very indirect in other aspects. It can take several meetings and conversations before you are able to broach the subject that you want to talk about. To race in soon after you have met a person would appear rude and show little tact, so you would be unlikely to get a favourable response. For instance, in business it is common to sit and chat about families, where you come from, how you have enjoyed your stay in Vietnam or general aspects of business before you discuss the specific issues that the meeting has been arranged for. If you know the family well, it is polite to ask about the health of each family member, starting with the eldest son and finishing with the youngest daughter.

Avoiding Issues

The pressures for social harmony are very strong. White lies are often told to ensure that no one gets upset. This avoidance of an issue often raises problems for foreigners. For instance, you may ask if a person is married as it sets the stage for later questions about his or her family. But if a woman tells you that her husband has died, do not ask how or when. It may be that he has left her for another woman and she saves face by giving such an answer. What she really means is that he is dead where her heart is concerned.

Yes and No

As in many Asian countries, a direct "no" is rarely given. People are more likely to smile and nod, change the subject or avoid discussing an issue altogether if the topic is unpleasant. A question that they find difficult to answer may be misunderstood on purpose so that they do not have to give you an answer that will upset you. In answer to a direct question, a "yes" probably means "maybe", "maybe" means "no" and

a "no", when actually spoken, means that under no circumstance will it occur. Learn to ask open-ended questions rather than closed ones requiring a "yes" or "no" answer. As the Vietnamese language often phrases questions in a negative form, an affirmative answer means "no". For instance, someone may ask you "Are you not going?" A "yes" answer means "I'm not going" and a "no" answer, means "I am going". This adds greatly to the confusion surrounding "yes" and "no" answers when conducted in poor English or Vietnamese!

Modesty

In conversation, people display great modesty towards their abilities and work. It is not acceptable to boast about one's past achievements or capabilities and, compared with foreigners, the Vietnamese often sound shy and reserved and are self-effacing about their own skills. Bearing this in mind, do not underestimate a person or assume that he is of low status. If your subsequent actions show a lack of regard for him, he will lose face.

Sense of Humour

The Vietnamese have a very good sense of humour that surfaces often. Their theatre, water puppet plays, woodcut block prints and

151

poetry all reflect this. The humour can be quite slapstick and, far more than most other Asian races, it can also be quite sarcastic. Aspects of it are very European and foreigners find the Vietnamese brand of humour quite easy to relate to. The people are witty and enjoy using their language to make a play on words. However, jokes in a foreign language may not be fully comprehended and you will often find that they laugh at your joke out of courtesy, even though they do not understand it. Avoid practical jokes, though. If they backfire, you may cause someone to lose face.

Display of Emotions

Emotions are displayed at all levels of communication, even when sign language is used. The Vietnamese are always very polite, even if only superficially, and they read a person's tone of voice and body language to get different messages. This can cause problems. For instance, if you are in a hurry and use rapid, direct speech to order people to get tasks done quickly to a deadline, they may infer from the tone and direct manner that you are upset with them.

Anger

If you get angry and raise your voice, you will often find people smiling or tittering to themselves. It is not that they find your behaviour funny, but they are embarrassed for you. You have displayed a weakness by becoming angry. Allowing it to surface is considered poor manners and is not the hallmark of a well-educated person. Anger directed at someone is taken as a direct criticism to be avoided at all costs. It may also be in a context that the Vietnamese do not understand. For instance, they are used to bureaucracy and do not always realise that you may find it unusual or unacceptable.

You may find yourself demanding that the hotel receptionist issue you with a receipt for your passport which she is keeping overnight. She cannot or will not and as your voice rises in anger and frustration, her expression turns blank and her face becomes wooden. This indicates that as far as she is concerned, you have passed the point of no return. She is embarrassed as you have caused her to lose face. Once you have reached this stage, you will receive no further assistance, cooperation or response from her. You can avert the situation by adopting a light-hearted approach, joking about the need for a receipt or spending time chatting with her. Accept that things are done quite differently in Vietnam and that all hotels retain passports and rarely issue receipts.

Be creative in your solutions. If you say "I'm so angry that this wasn't completed during my absence ...", you will meet with avoidance and denial. But say "I'm so disappointed. I had really hoped that we'd be able to get this done by now..." and there will be a flurry of activity while everyone works as a team to try to finish the task. This technique is a tried and tested approach that works, if you are prepared to control your anger!

As with any other race of people, the Vietnamese can get angry too. They may actually fly into a towering rage. This happens only when the matter is very serious and such behaviour is usually seen only among the lower classes of people. The better-educated will suppress their anger or, at least, not show it in public if possible. Instead, they may talk in a small group and reason through their anger, particularly if it is directed at a certain person, action or behaviour.

HOW TO LEARN

You will meet many people who are happy to trade English lessons for Vietnamese lessons. This can work out very well for both parties. Besides learning a language, you invariably learn a great deal more as well. This includes social etiquette and information about the people and country. However, not everyone is cut out to be a good teacher. It may help to buy a "How to learn Vietnamese" book to give the lessons some structure. Phrasebooks and dictionaries are readily available in Vietnam, but well-structured teaching books are not at present. So bring one with you.

If you are serious about learning the language, there are qualified teachers who give lessons for a little cash. You can choose to have your lessons in a group or on your own. A cheaper alternative may be to learn at a university. There are educational establishments in Ho Chi Minh City and Hanoi that run very good, intensive courses.

As you start to learn, a whole new world will open up before you and you will quickly make new friends. Still, take care in using new words. The more you know, the more traps you may fall into. For instance, there are many ways of saying "he" or "she". Each has its own subtle nuances which may be positive or negative.

Chapter Seven

SOCIALISING IN VIETNAM

Anyone who visits Vietnam, even for a short period, cannot help but notice the ceremonies and festivals that seem to occur almost endlessly. These are part and parcel of the people's lifestyle. A basic understanding of them will make the events more enjoyable. As you acquire Vietnamese friends, either through work or in social circles, you will start receiving invitations to dinners, weddings or other outings. There is a definite protocol concerning behaviour in some of these circumstances and, to a Vietnamese, there are many subtle nuances that can be read from another person's behaviour. Fortunately for a foreign visitor, things are not too complicated. At the basic level, a smile, courtesy, the display of good intentions and deference to elders will get you through most situations. Despite this, specific things will be expected of you during certain festivals and celebrations and the most important of these are covered here, together with general dos and don'ts. Appropriate behaviour during greetings, introductions and conversations have been covered in Chapter 6, Communication.

SOCIAL ETIQUETTE

The strongest unwritten rule is that everyone works hard to create and maintain social harmony. Self-discipline is regarded as a virtue and a sign of a good background. Because of this, you will not find people arguing, raising their voices or getting angry as much as in other societies. Unpleasant subjects will simply be avoided or talked around. It can be very difficult for you to find out that some of your actions are inappropriate or unacceptable to the people—no one is willing to tell you, fearing that it may upset you. People do not want to break bad news to you either. This is often manifested by people leaving the room or being uncontactable when something has gone wrong.

The Vietnamese do not brag and, instead, it is polite to be self-deprecatory, a habit not followed by many Westerners. Direct eye contact is avoided. In more traditional areas, a person often speaks while covering his mouth with his hand or something else that is handy. This is especially so when a man speaks to a young woman. It is impolite for the man to look directly at her until he gets to know her better. Young children and men, however, can be addressed in a direct manner. See Chapter 6, Communication for more information about conversations and non-verbal language.

The elderly are shown great respect and you should always greet the oldest first, allow him or her to go ahead of you and generally take your cue from the person's actions. This applies to most occasions unless you happen to be the guest of honour, in which case you will be encouraged to go first during a ceremony. Religious statues and pictures of venerated political figures should not be treated lightly. Some Westerners shocked their staff by placing a hat on the bust of Ho Chi Minh that was in their house and were politely requested to remove it.

GIFT-GIVING

Presents are given on numerous occasions. If you call at a friend's house for dinner, or someone is celebrating a birthday, it is appropriate to take along a small present such as fruits, flowers or a plant. When you return from a trip, it is common to bring back a token of friendship, such as a box of chocolates or T-shirts for your staff. Gift-giving is very much a part of certain celebrations such as Tet, or a wedding. The appropriate type of present and how it should be delivered is covered in the relevant sections in this chapter.

In the West, a gift is a symbol of thanks from the giver. In Vietnam, where Buddhism prevails, giving a gift is one way in which the giver can gain greater merit for the next life. Hence, the whole action is to the benefit of the giver, not the receiver. The Vietnamese will not open your gift in front of you but will accept it, place it aside and open it later. While they may thank you upon receipt of the present, do not expect a subsequent thanks once the contents have been unwrapped and examined. The acknowledgement will not be forthcoming.

Colours and animals can have symbolic meanings which are worth remembering during the selection of gifts. Red is warm and is always a good colour; purple is feminine and romantic; green is youthful; blue is linked with freshness, love and hope; black is associated with mourning, unhappiness and gloom; and white with death and funerals. However, white also means purity. Young women wear white *ao dais* and white roses are a perfect gift for a young girl's birthday. So, too, are the large, white fragrant narcissus, or *hoa cuc,* that symbolise success and prosperity. Yellow is a confusing colour. It is seen a lot at Tet (as a substitute for gold). Yellow flowering plants are fine then and yellow wedding dresses can be seen, but yellow flowers are never given for a birthday as they are associated with betrayal.

Turtles are a display of endurance, strength and longevity; dragons represent good luck and fortune; a crane signifies fidelity and longevity as it is the bird sent from heaven to fetch people destined for eternal life; spiders are a lucky sign with regard to money; and a buffalo symbolises patience and loyalty. But a cow is stupid, a pig both lazy and stupid, a monkey bad, and a raven or owl an omen of death and definitely not suitable as a present if depicted in a picture or ornament.

You will need to be careful about certain types of gifts. Most flowers are fine but avoid hue. These have hundreds of tiny, white flowers at the top of tall stems and are usually used at altars. Chrysanthemums are usually reserved for funeral wreaths. Pink roses are for lovers. The Vietnamese word for handkerchief, *khan,* is associated with the word *kho,* meaning "difficulty". *Kho khan* means hardship, so handkerchiefs are not given as presents. Young girls used to embroider their name on the corner of one and give it to their boyfriends when the latter departed for war. Many young men never returned and handkerchiefs have come to be regarded as a symbol of grief and parting. Knives stand for fighting. Gifts of perfume, deodorant or soap mean that you think the person smells.

Not everyone is superstitious and many modern women appreciate imported gifts of perfume or cosmetics, but be careful about giving them. Chocolates or other imported foods are also popular and can be shared around in an office, as can fashion magazines. For men, ties, tiepins, pens, shirts, cigarettes and whisky are always welcome. Cognac is sipped rather than drunk fast and tends to carry a higher status than whisky. You can always ask a friend what he or she would like you to get from your scheduled trip abroad. Do not be surprised if you get a specific answer such as a cream-coloured handbag of a certain size to go with a special outfit. However, the better-educated

Vietnamese who have been exposed to foreign ways may not be so forthcoming as they know that it is not polite in many foreign cultures to ask for presents. A general rule is that any imported item not easily obtainable in Vietnam is fine!

Make sure the gifts are obviously from another country. One businessman gave a small lacquered box from Malaysia to a member of his staff, who queried him on whether it was bought in Vietnam or overseas. While the design was obviously Malaysian, lacquerware is very common in Vietnam and the present was not as well appreciated as would something that is unobtainable in the country.

FESTIVALS AND HOLIDAYS

There are many special days in the Vietnamese calendar. Some of these are based on the Gregorian calendar (the solar calendar) and others on the lunar calendar, which means that their corresponding dates on the Gregorian calendar alter slightly each year. The Vietnamese lunar calendar began in the year 2637 B.C., as did the Chinese calendar, and each month has either 29 or 30 days, with a total of 355 days a year. Every three years, an additional month is added between the third and fourth months so that the pace between the lunar and Gregorian calendars is maintained.

Each festival has its own set of ceremonies and traditions. Some celebrations only involve close family members but others are enjoyed by everyone. At times, you will see banners, parades, ceremonies, and traditional foods and gifts lining the streets. The traditions surrounding each festival would take a whole book to explain, so only a brief description of the more important ones has been included here. Those that are official public holidays are indicated as such.

Special Days on the Gregorian Calendar

January 1	New Year's Day, a public holiday
February 3	Establishment of the Vietnamese Communist Party in 1930, a public holiday.

March 8	International Women's Day, established in 1911. You can give flowers to female employees.
March 26	Establishment of the Ho Chi Minh Communist Youth Organisation in 1931.
April 25	General election for the Unified Vietnamese Assembly, started in 1976.
April 30	Liberation of South Vietnam, a public holiday.
May 1	International Labour Day, a public holiday.
May 19	The anniversary of Ho Chi Minh's birthday, a public holiday.
June 1	International Children's Day. Organisations may hold functions for children and give them small gifts.
July 2	In 1976, Vietnam was named the Socialist Republic of Vietnam by the Sixth National Assembly.
July 20	The signing date of the Geneva Treaty in 1954.
July 27	War Invalids and War Deaths Day. Ceremonial visits to cemeteries are optional.
September 2	Vietnam National Day. Also known as Independence Day, this celebrates the founding of the nation by Ho Chi Minh in 1945 and is a public holiday. You can send flowers, gifts or cards to relevant state authorities. Some Vietnamese companies pay out an additional staff bonus on this day.
September 3	The anniversary of Ho Chi Minh's death in 1969. He actually died on September 2, which was already celebrated as National Day, so the death was not announced until the next day.
October 20	Establishment of the Vietnam Women's Federal Association in 1930.
November 20	Vietnamese Teachers' Day. Send a gift, such as flowers and a card, to your children's teachers.
December 25	Christmas Day, a public holiday. Gifts and cards should be sent to the relevant state authorities.

Special Days Based on the Lunar Year

There are many more, but the following are the more important celebrations. To be sure you get the dates correct, buy a calendar which indicates the lunar festivals and their corresponding dates on a Gregorian calendar.

1st–7th of the first month	Tet, the Vietnamese New Year's Day. This usually occurs between late January and mid-February. It is the most important event in the whole year and is dealt with in a subsequent section. A public holiday stretching over a minimum of three days is enjoyed and it is a time of fun, festivals, joyous celebrations and gift-giving.
8th–9th of the first month	People go to the pagoda to worship.
15th of the first month	*Le Thuong Nguon.* People visit the pagoda.
3rd of the third month	This is a time when cold foods are eaten.
5th of the third month	*Thanh Minh.* The deceased are worshipped and graves tidied.
8th of the fourth month	*Phat Dan.* Buddha's birthday anniversary, a one-day public holiday that usually falls in June.
5th of the fifth month	*Tet Doan Ngu.* This is summer solstice, a celebration of the day when the sun is at its highest and vitality is believed to be at its peak. As it also marks the start of the decline towards winter, offerings are given to the spirits to keep away diseases. Effigies of humans are burnt to satisfy the god of death. People may take fruits at break-

161

fast to kill their intestinal worms, drop lemon juice in their eyes at noon to brighten them, or wash their hair at noon to make it shine.

15th of the seventh month

Trung Nguyen, or Wandering Souls Day, is the second most important festival after Tet. People will worship at home, often outside where the souls may be, or in temples and pagodas. The sins of the dead are forgiven and special prayers are said for all the dead who have no living descendants to worship them. Joss papers are burnt. Large amounts of food are prepared for the wandering souls and, after the worship ceremony, the food is often distributed to poor children.

15th of the eighth month

Trung Thu or mid-Autumn Tet. This is for children and special processions take place with decorative lanterns, dragon dances, gongs and drums. Special cakes and fruits are eaten. It is also known as mini-Tet and mooncakes or a toy are special presents given at this time.

28th of the ninth month

The anniversary of Confucius' birthday.

10th of the tenth month

Thong Tan Tet, or the harvest festival. People celebrate the end of harvest and give presents: children will give gifts to their parents, patients to their doctors, and pupils to their teachers, particularly in the south.

Other Special Days

There are many other special days, some associated with the observance of certain Buddhist rites, others with a specific locality and ancient festival. For instance, the fishermen of Vung Tau make offerings to the whale genie once a year. There is *Kate* for the Chams, the *Giong* festival in Gia Lam district, *Oc Om Boc* celebrated by the Khmers, the *Chu Dong Tu* festival in Hai Hung province, elephant racing at Dac Lac in spring or visits to the Perfume Pagoda, Chua Huong, after Tet. If you are travelling or want to witness special ceremonies, ask a tourist agent for more information.

Tet—Vietnamese New Year

The complete name is *Tet Nguyen Lan*. The word *Tet* is derived from *Tiet,* which means "festival", and as this is the grandest and most important occasion in the year, most people simply call it Tet. Originally of Chinese origin, it now is surrounded by Vietnamese traditions. It marks the equinox and therefore the beginning of spring and, for agrarian people, the start of the New Year. The preparations and celebrations used to be spread over three months but, in an effort to increase productivity, the government has limited the holiday period to three days! Still, you will find great excitement building up well before Tet. Enormous amounts of money and presents flood in from relatives based overseas and there is an air of prosperity, wealth and fun. People are kept busy cooking traditional foods, buying gifts and fireworks, and preparing for the New Year.

Anyone living in Vietnam over the Tet season will get caught up in the festivities. You will also be expected to join in. What you do and say can have great bearing and it is important to understand the significance of your actions so that you do not inadvertently cast bad luck on someone for the rest of the year. There are also certain obligations you should fulfil at this time. Work out with your staff well in advance on who among them wants to go home on holiday or visit relatives in another part of Vietnam. Because so many choose to

163

take their annual holiday at this time, some businesses are closed for longer than the holiday period prescribed by the government. If you want to get anything done on the business side, avoid doing it just before or after Tet. As the demand for goods increases rapidly in the buying spree, so do their prices, making it a very expensive time of the year. Some people even spend beyond their budget.

Domestic staff usually work out a roster among themselves for the Tet period. You may well be able to cope with diminished household help but you should ensure that you still have adequate security over this period. State your needs to the staff in advance so that they have time to work out suitable arrangements.

All your employees should receive extra money, approximately an additional month's salary, placed in their New Year card. It should be given a week or two before Tet to ensure that they have sufficient cash to buy presents for relatives and friends. It is also traditional to give lucky money, *li xi*. A crisp, new note, never an old one, must be placed in a small red envelope that can be bought in stationery stores. These are given to children or to people extremely subordinate to you. For instance, if your secretary has three children, you should give her three *li xi* packets, one for each child. The amount of money given is quite small, but is a symbol of the fortune of the giver as well as how close you are to the recipient.

You must also give gifts. These are a symbol of friendship and show that you care about the recipient. Everyone in your employment and those whom you have regular contact with, or who have helped you previously, should get a gift and a special Tet card. Certain items are deemed to bring good luck in the New Year. Tea, candies, dried sausages, fruits, plants and flowers are all suitable. Fruiting kumquat trees, candied ginger, crystallised coconut and candied lotus seeds are good. Peach and apricot tree branches symbolise the start of the New Year and are thought to help provide protection from evil spirits. The pink peach is best for a northerner and the yellow apricot for a southerner (try not to give pink to a southerner or yellow to a northerner even if they are living in the south). Red and yellow flowers are ideal as they make the house more welcoming to good spirits.

Prior to Tet, the streets are full of traditional gift items that are up for sale, so you will not have any trouble locating them. As a foreigner, though, you may prefer to give something else. This is acceptable as it will be understood that you mean well and the thought is there, but remember that your gift will not have the traditional associations with good luck. Considering this, it may be better to save such gifts for another occasion. But because of all the merrymaking that occurs during Tet, bottles of whisky, while less traditional, are now quite acceptable. Similarly, champagne has gained ready acceptance as a celebratory drink as its cork pops off, sounding like fireworks, a traditional part of any Tet celebration. Do not give a Tet present that is white, and do not wrap a present in white paper or with a white bow. White is the colour associated with death and funerals. Red and gold (or yellow) will bring good luck for the following year. As usual, there are exceptions as the white narcissus flowers, which smell so sweet, are perfectly acceptable!

Tet Foods

Each household purchases a pair of watermelons. The redder the colour inside, the better luck the household will have in the following year. Traditionally, no food can be cooked over Tet so dried foods and cold food that can keep without refrigeration must be prepared for the huge feasts that occur. For instance, *banh chung* is made from ordinary foods—sticky rice, yellow mung beans and fatty pork—but its preparation is time-consuming. The rice is first soaked for 24 hours and then the mixture is made, wrapped in banana leaf and steamed for another 24–48 hours (see Chapter 9, Eating Vietnamese Food).

When to Give Presents

Presents are usually taken around to friends' houses a couple of days prior to Tet. This way, people know what you are giving them and do not have to spend money buying the same items. An alternative is to give the present at the last moment, just prior to Tet, so that it is too late for the other party to reciprocate, and he will not lose face for not giving you a gift in return. Most Vietnamese friends understand that you merely want to help them enjoy their New Year, which is not your New Year, so they need not reciprocate with a present for you. But it can be a good idea to say so directly if you have the opportunity, particularly if you feel your friend may have stretched his finances at this time.

Timetable

In the month or two prior to Tet, new clothes will be purchased, gifts bought, the kitchen stocked and the whole house cleaned and up-graded if possible. This is the time when many household items receive a new coat of paint. It is a time to settle all the problems of the past year so that luck and good fortune will be with you in the New Year. People try to forget past sins and start the New Year with no enemies. Debts will be paid off so that they can start on a clean slate. Some flock in from the country to visit relatives. Prices rise and pickpockets and thieves are very active, so this is a good time to avoid shopping in crowded places.

The Vietnamese believe that every kitchen is inhabited by a kitchen god, or *tao quan*. The gods watch over their respective households throughout the year and, on the 23rd day of the 12th lunar month, go to heaven to report to the Jade Emperor on the merits and failings of the families that they live with. People aid the gods' journey by making incense and food offerings prior to their departure. A live carp is used as it is believed to be able to transport the kitchen gods to heaven. The gods are not deemed to be infallible, however, and offerings of whisky are given to them so that they will end up in heaven drunk and only remember the good things about the family. On this day, your office staff may go out for lunch together or arrange a dinner to celebrate. *Tat Nien* is held on the last afternoon before the New Year commences. A sacrifice is held for the ancestors to welcome their souls back to earth for three days to join in the Tet celebrations.

At midnight, *Giao Thua* starts and everyone must be at home by the ancestral shrine or at a pagoda. At this time, the kitchen gods of the past year are thanked for the care they have provided and the new kitchen gods who will arrive for the coming year are welcomed. While few people still believe in the kitchen gods, the traditions surrounding them are firmly entrenched in their folklore and celebrated.

During the absence of the kitchen gods and before the arrival of the new ones, the occupants of each house lack the usual protection from evil spirits, so noise is used to scare the bad genies away. Hence, Tet is known as a time of endless noise. Lights are left on inside the house for the same reason. Do not expect to get much sleep over this period. As the clock rolls past midnight and into the beginning of the New Year, the firecrackers start and the deafening noise does not stop! Many of the firecrackers are large and it is easy to see why the 1968 Tet Offensive, when the Viet Cong pushed into what was then Saigon, was so successful. The fireworks of Tet sound just like guns and grenades so the extra sounds were not noticed. Be careful, though, and watch over yourself and your belongings. Hundreds of people are injured every year from burns and dozens lose their lives because of these firecrackers. Some of the fireworks have been known to make small craters in roads, others are carelessly thrown and small ones tossed to make you jump as you walk by. It is a good time to keep yourself and your pets indoors. Because of the economic costs and disruption that the firecrackers cause, the government has decided to ban the private purchase of fireworks for future Tets. Fireworks are made in Vietnam and also smuggled in from China, so how successful the ban is remains to be seen.

The First Day of Tet

Everyone gets up early. The first sound heard has special meaning. For instance, a cock crowing means hard work and a bad harvest for the rest of the year, but a dog barking means confidence and trust. Only good comments and well wishes can be spoken all day. To do otherwise would be to wish a whole year's bad luck on someone. Food offerings are put out for the kitchen gods every morning and evening for three days. Children receive their *li xi,* or red envelopes with "lucky" money inside. Visits to family members and friends are planned. This is done very carefully as the first visitor to cross the threshold of a house will bring all their good or bad luck with them and this will remain in the house for the rest of the year. The happiness, status, parentage, wealth, number of children, frame of mind as well as luck of the person are all taken into account. The first visitor is rarely left to chance and usually coordinated in advance. People visit the pagoda and bring back the branch of a plant as a symbol of happiness. No housework is done over Tet. Not even the kitchen floor can be swept in case the good spirits are tossed out.

Day 2

Games and various forms of entertainment are staged and these often last a week. Different regions have varying specialities but they may include wrestling, buffalo fighting or dancing.

Day 3

A ceremony is held to honour the dead as they return to their world. Graves are often visited as people escort their ancestors back to their resting place. The streets get busy. Traffic reduces to a snarl and it is a time when many foreigners go overseas to escape the noise for a few days. However, it is also a very exciting time and great for photography. Everyone should experience the celebrations of Tet at least once. It is a time of fun, festivals and fairs throughout the country.

Foreigners in the country should show their appreciation of

friends and send the appropriate cards and gifts to their Vietnamese associates. You may receive invitations to visit but remember that Tet is a time when families get together. Unless you are sure they really want your presence and are not just being polite, you need not attend. If you do, visitors are expected to pay their respects to the dead as well as to the living, and this is done at the family shrine when you first enter the house. Do not go if you have recently had any bad luck—a death in the family or a divorce, or if you are pregnant.

WEDDINGS

Weddings are occasions that bring family and friends together. Invitations to weddings are something to look forward to. Most weddings occur after the rainy season and prior to Tet. The rice has already been harvested so food is plentiful and the sun is out, which makes it a better time for photography. The ceremonies differ a little depending on the region, how traditional the people are and how much they can afford to spend.

These days, couples fall in love and decide to get married but arranged marriages still occur. Parental approval is sought by almost all couples before they wed. This is sometimes withheld, even if the two are in love, because of perceived incompatibility between the families due to educational status, social rank or cultural differences. The birthdays of proposed brides and grooms must also be checked against each other to ensure that their horoscopes are compatible and that the match is a fortunate one. At the first formal meeting between the two families, the date and place for the betrothal ceremony are set.

The betrothal ceremony starts with a procession of people from the boy's family arriving at the girl's house. They bear gifts packed in special red wedding boxes covered with red cloth. An essential part of the gifts is a large bunch of areca nuts and betel leaves as these are a traditional symbol of conjugal love. Gold for the bride in the form of a ring, necklace, bracelet and earrings should be included to show the wealth of the prospective groom. Also included are a big basket

Western-style wedding gowns are just as popular as traditional bridal outfits.

of fruit, two large candles for the family altar, a special cake *(banh com)* and, perhaps, a couple of bottles of whisky.

While still outside the house, the boy's family asks the girl's family for permission for the wedding. The male members of the girl's family go outside to check the presents. If these are accepted, permission is granted for the wedding and the groom's family may enter the house. A small party is held to celebrate. The older men drink rice wine together and agree on the union and then the older women from both families do the same. A fortune teller must be consulted to work out the most auspicious date and time for the wedding. It may be held as early as 2 a.m. and perhaps in only a month's time or, more traditionally, up to three years later. If there has been a recent death in the family it is considered appropriate to wait for a reasonable period of time.

The gifts will be divided into two uneven piles. The smaller one is given back to the groom's family to show that they have been overly generous with their gifts. This also serves to formalise the ties. The edible items in the larger pile will be distributed to the bride's family and friends.

Invitations are sent out one week to 10 days before the wedding. You may be invited only to the afternoon reception or to an earlier family party as well. The day before the wedding, both the bride and groom may also hold separate parties with their friends.

Proceedings vary a little but on the day of the wedding, a delegation from the groom's family goes to the bride's house, headed by a master of ceremonies, or *chu hon*. When they arrive, firecrackers are let off before the groom's family enters the bride's house. The bridegroom and his attendants go to the bridal chamber and present a bouquet to the bride, who then emerges. The gift of jewellery from the groom will be put on her, the two big candles will be lit and whisky will be consumed, together with foods for special occasions. including cake. These days, lots of photographs are taken and, perhaps, a video recording of the whole procedure as well. It is not unusual for this part to take up to three hours. The bride is then escorted to the groom's family home for the actual reception although these days, this may take place in a restaurant instead.

Decorated cars then take the group to the wedding reception. The bridal group then welcomes each of the guests and after all have arrived, firecrackers are let off again and the obligatory speeches will begin. The *chu hon* makes the speeches, welcoming the guests and thanking them for their attendance. Brides often hire the clothes that they wear and it is usual for a bride to change her gown several times during the reception. Each change is a status symbol showing how much money has been spent. Each new dress calls for more photos and for people to admire how beautiful she looks in the new style. If you attend a wedding, try not to be more showy or more beautiful than the bride as such action is considered to be in poor taste.

If you had been invited to the earlier family celebrations as well, you would have given your gift there. If not, it is given when the bride and groom, and their parents, call personally at each table (about one hour after everyone has started eating). They make a short speech thanking their guests for attending and this is the time to present your gift to the groom while wishing him luck and fortune for the bridal union. If you cannot attend the wedding, send the present in advance. Close friends and relatives will give an envelope containing money. This is often preferred as the couple can then buy what they need. If you take a gift, it should obviously be an imported one, if possible, and wrapped very nicely (avoid white paper or ribbon). Traditionally, it is better to give a pair of items rather than a single present, which was thought to indicate that the marriage would not last long. These days, however, few follow this practice.

At this point, dancing may be introduced and the whole reception may take at least five hours before the bride and groom leave for the groom's home. It is considered bad luck if the couple do not spend at least the first night in the house of the groom's father. If the wedding is in a different location, the father must rent a house which acts as a substitute for his.

The formal signing of government marriage papers can be done either before or after the wedding ceremony and the timing is not crucial. It can be six months after the ceremonies, for instance, but most people prefer to do it before the birth of their first baby to avoid any problems. The local policeman must countersign the papers as it is assumed that he knows the two people and can attest that they are not already married to someone else. If one party lives elsewhere, his or her local policeman must also sign the papers.

Historically, the whole marriage process was not easy for either side. The prospective groom was expected to attend to the family of the bride months in advance of the actual wedding, helping around the house and doing whatever they asked. This could include going daily to the well and fetching water. It was a time to test the seriousness of the groom's intentions as well as his ability to work hard and look after the bride well. After the couple were married, the wife would live with the husband's family for between one and three years (traditionally three) to demonstrate to the mother-in-law that she knew how to care for the son properly. The husband would always be fed first, followed by the children and, lastly, the wife herself. After this, if the couple could afford it, they would move into their own home. This period in the husband's household also bonded the wife to her new family. Many still follow this last practice partly for economic reasons, but there are several stories of the new wife being treated very poorly, more like a slave.

In the past, a boy living in a rural area would marry at the age of 16 or 17 and a girl at 14 or 15. In the city, the people marry a little later. However, marriage is occurring at a much later age now. City teenagers feel the need to be established before they settle down. Boys may wait until their late twenties, when they have completed their education and worked for several years, so that they can afford a house and motorcycle before settling down.

A NEW CHILD

Children are very important and boys are regarded as special as they carry on the family lineage and play an important role in ancestral worship. Girls will marry into another family and be "lost".

For the first month after a baby is born, mother and child observe a period of home confinement called *day thang*. After this, a family celebration is held and presents are given to the godmother, whose role it is to protect the child and teach it to smile. Its first birthday, described as "quitting the cradle", is more important than all subsequent birthdays so a large party is usually held. A gift of a gold ring, bracelet or chain for the child is favoured traditionally but a toy or clothes for the child are also suitable, as is alcohol for the celebrations.

FUNERALS

Buddhists believe in reincarnation so the attitude displayed at a funeral can confuse a Westerner. While it is a time of mourning it is also a time to prepare the soul for the journey to a new life, which may be a better one. Where a person dies is very important and if someone is very ill in hospital, the family will bring him home quickly so that he can die in the appropriate place. After a person dies, the body may be kept for a few days to give relatives living in other areas sufficient time to arrive for the funeral. It may be kept at home or, if the house is too small, pagodas have a special room for this purpose. The mourning rites are then performed at an altar that is specially set up for the occasion.

This is followed by a large, expensive procession. A special vehicle to carry the casket is hired, together with funeral clothes, musicians, attendants and many other items. Mourners wear black and white as they follow the casket through the streets on its way to its final resting place. White head scarves are a sign of mourning and close relatives often dress very poorly in cheap, white sack-like clothes to indicate their lack of caring for their image because of their intense grief. Someone in the party may hold a photo of the deceased. The body may either be cremated or buried depending on the wishes of the deceased. Specific burial locations are often decided with the aid of a geomancer, hence graves are seen scattered through the countryside in odd places.

The period of mourning observed by relatives of the deceased

Funerals are elaborate and street processions are a traditional part of the ceremony.

varies, depending on their relationship to the dead person. During this time, they should not visit pagodas, attend festivals, marry or wear bright colours. As a sign of mourning, men wear a black arm band and women have a small piece of black cloth attached to their outfit. After a few years, usually three, the body will be exhumed from its grave and the bones are rearranged into a small earthenware container and taken to the family's ancestral land. So, too, the urns of those cremated may be moved but both practices are not strictly observed these days as the mobility of people over the past 40–50 years means that fewer have been able to retain their traditional family land. Some move to the cities and others go overseas.

If you are invited to a funeral, it is polite to send flowers or a wreath, and a condolence card, but it is not essential that you attend in person. Find out where the actual rites are to be held as the wreath must go there. It is an ill omen to send it to the house of mourning if the rites are not being held there. If you are wearing a hat when a funeral procession passes you on the street, you can stop and take off your hat until the procession has gone by. This gesture is simply a mark of respect but is rarely observed now in busy cities such as Ho Chi Minh City, although it is still practised in the country.

DEATH ANNIVERSARY

This is a family affair when relatives get together to remember an ancestor. Each person brings food for the meal they will share and all help in the cooking. Friends are not usually invited and if you are, a polite refusal will be accepted. However, if you wish to attend, food is the best gift.

HOSTING VIETNAMESE

It is common courtesy for Vietnamese families to serve a drink, and perhaps some fruit, when guests arrive, instead of asking if they would care for a drink as is the practice in the West. Vietnamese women tend not to drink much coffee, although the men do, so tea, fruit juice or a soft drink are more appropriate.

Traditionally, the Vietnamese do not reply to invitations. Many do not have telephones and the mail can take too long so people may or may not turn up at a wedding or function, depending on their mood at the time. Most functions used to be held privately and food was provided buffet-style, so exact numbers were not very important. Increasingly, as the people become more familiar with foreign ways, they respect the need to know in advance how many people will be attending. These days, they also do more entertaining at restaurants so the Vietnamese hosts themselves need to know the numbers to be catered for. Despite this, do not expect the people to commit themselves in advance when it comes to accepting invitations to functions.

Try to find out about your guests beforehand. Are they Buddhists or Christians? Many Vietnamese will say they are Buddhist but are not devout, so this will not always be a problem. You may choose to serve a buffet and label vegetarian dishes clearly so that there will be no dietary issues. It also allows the people to select how much or how little of each dish they may want. You should not serve rich, creamy or cheesy sauces. Most Vietnamese do not like this type of food and it may actually make them sick. A little butter is all right as are spicy foods. The Vietnamese do not usually eat dessert and fresh fruit is often a better substitute.

Visiting Vietnamese Friends

Apart from festival time and special occasions, you may be invited for dinner or asked to drop by for a chat. Take a small gift, perhaps of some fruit. Dress neatly as a sign of respect for your host, but do not overdress for the occasion. Read Chapter 6, Communication for appropriate greetings, conversation and body language. While the Vietnamese generally do not give an RSVP to your invitation, or else say they will come and do not turn up, do not treat them the same way. You may well be the intended guest of honour at their meal or function. The Vietnamese are punctual during functions so do turn up on time.

Do not be surprised when you visit their house as the Vietnamese standard of living is much lower than what you may be accustomed to. Even a person holding a good job may live in a small, old house with several members of his extended family. Privacy is minimal. City apartments or even country houses may have only two or three rooms, plus a kitchen and toilet area. Because of this, people will move out onto a balcony or the street to do their daily toilet such as combing their hair. Rooms are multi-functional and furniture is kept to a minimum. Chairs and tables tend to be of a lower height than what most foreigners are used to. A kitchen will usually be located at the rear or side of a house. Cooking is often done over a charcoal stove rather than one powered by gas or electricity.

Do not drop by for a casual visit even if you have been told to do so. Telephone first or make an arrangement to go at a certain time. If you drop by unexpectedly, many Vietnamese may be embarrassed that their house is not tidy or that they do not have something to offer you. Lunch traditionally includes a siesta time so do not visit between noon and 1.30 p.m. unless your host has specifically suggested it. Always follow his lead. If he slips off his shoes as he enters the house, do likewise. Unlike in the West where you may be offered a drink, a drink will always be brought to you whether you are thirsty or not. Usually, it will be tea, water or a fruit juice. You do not have to finish the drink. It is polite to drink a little but if you empty the glass or cup, your host is obliged to refill it.

Eating with the Vietnamese

If a southern family offers you food, it is most impolite not to join them. If you are not hungry, just explain that you have eaten recently, then sit with them and chat as they eat. You should take a small amount yourself and enjoy it. It is an insult to the host to refuse his food altogether. To make things rather confusing for the foreigner, the tradition of the northern people is just the reverse. You should refuse an invitation to join them for a meal unless it has been repeated many times. This custom came about because, in the past, people from the north had little food and no resources to feed an extra mouth. So while the invitation was extended out of courtesy, you were expected to refuse it.

Chapter 9 explains Vietnamese food, eating habits and appropriate behaviour in greater detail. Be prepared to make an impromptu thank-you speech sometime during the meal. If they ask you what you would like to drink, be very careful not to embarrass them by asking for something they may not have. Even those who are quite well-off rarely stock soft drinks and it is safest to ask for tea, coffee or water. The family may not have any milk and alcohol is rarely drunk at home.

Eating Out

If you invite someone out for lunch or dinner, you must pay for the meal. Younger Vietnamese are more inclined to go out with friends for casual dinner outings and are prepared to split the bill accordingly. In family situations, the most senior person present pays.

DATING A VIETNAMESE

Partnerships between locals and foreigners can and do occur. The relationship is usually between a Vietnamese girl and a foreign man and this is a lot rockier than the other way around. Girls are expected to be virgins when they marry and their moral character is very important. More traditional families may not like a liaison with a foreigner. Western morals are seen as very low. As a foreigner, you can expect to be chaperoned on your dates, perhaps by a brother or cousin. If you are serious, take small gifts for the family and spend time with them as a Vietnamese man would.

Beware if you start a liaison that may not be easy to break without repercussions. There are many poorer-class Vietnamese who would like to marry a foreigner because it would enable them to leave Vietnam and enjoy better living conditions elsewhere. It is seen as a path to wealth. Families of the Vietnamese partner may feel slighted if the relationship is called off. They may ask for money but can also cause other problems for you, such as bureaucratic (if the family has government connections) and physical attacks.

Couples who fall in love and wish to marry will face many problems. They can live together legally before they marry but bureaucracy and the social stigma can make it very hard. Vietnamese women who go out with foreign men are generally treated very poorly by other Vietnamese—particularly the men. Unless she comes from a privileged background, they normally assume that she is a prostitute or bargirl as she would not otherwise have met the man! Once the social problems have been overcomed, however, couples can marry with relative ease and the appropriate passport for the new wife can be obtained.

SUPERSTITIONS

There are literally thousands of superstitions in Vietnam, many derived from animism and ancestral worship. The visitor will find it impossible to learn about and remember all of them as they vary from region to region. The younger generation tend not to believe in many of the superstitions but if you are in doubt about your actions, ask a Vietnamese. Remember to make it an open-ended question as they are unlikely to give you a definite "yes" or "no" answer.

Most of the traditional beliefs will not affect you. For instance, the Vietnamese believe that children should not eat bananas or eggs on the day of an examination, and it is considered bad luck to break a bottle of fish sauce or find a cat straying into your house. Yet it is good luck to see a dog come into the house, to pass a funeral, or to dream of fire or those who are dead. Some of your actions, however, may cause problems. For instance, it is considered bad luck to take photographs of three people. Expect trouble if you try this as three is an unlucky number. If you are pregnant, try not to block the way of someone leaving their house for a trip, business or examination as you will be blamed for their failure.

Shopkeepers often believe that their business luck is dependent on the first customer of the day or month. Foreigners may be welcome as they tend to pay good prices, but only if they understand that they must buy the first item that they pick up and examine. If you do not want to feel obliged to buy, you should avoid shopping early. Otherwise, expect the shopkeepers to be very rude towards you as they will blame you for subsequent bad luck and poor business.

Superstitions regarding numbers are very strong. They affect everything, from determining the opening date for shops and the starting date for a task to moving into a new home and the choice of whom you should marry. There are variations in beliefs. A person's lucky numbers are calculated by a numerologist. Such numbers are based on the time, day and year in which the person was born. It is generally held that 13 is unlucky (as in the West) and nine is lucky (as for the Chinese). Three is not a good number and many people will not undertake a new task on the 13th or 23rd day of a lunar month. Combinations of numbers are also important and people will try to avoid number plates, telephone numbers or identification numbers that appear unlucky.

Before setting the date for a major project or occasion, check a lunar calendar for an auspicious date. It is used for determining good days and bad days for starting a trip, embarking on a new business, opening a hotel, getting married or anything else where a successful outcome may depend on some measure of luck. You can buy calendars that indicate what should or should not be done on a particular day (and at what hour of the day). While you may not believe in it, it is worth bearing in mind that your staff or customers may, and that many foreign businesses make it a point to select appropriate days for important functions or the commencement of new business.

RELAXATION

Few people have much relaxation time. Everyone has to work hard to make ends meet or strive for a better life. Children will work in the family business, help with chores or take on an extra job like shining shoes. Men and women often have more than one job so when one finishes, the next starts. The elderly will be baby-sitting or helping with chores too. The unemployed or those doing a few casual jobs have the most time on their hands but, of course, no money to enjoy it with. Spare time may be spent playing with children or, in the case of city dwellers, taking them to a park.

Sitting and gossiping with friends in a street cafe over coffee, tea or maybe a beer is one of the main leisure activities for men. Small sidewalk stalls can be seen everywhere. Some provide entertainment with a television set or video. Few women are seen at these places as they generally work more hours a day, attending to household chores as well as earning a living outside the home.

The cinemas are generally losing their popularity as videos are more commonly available now. Modern youngsters spend their time courting, cruising the streets on a bicycle or, more recently, on motorcycles, dressed in Western gear. They assemble at favourite road intersections and families join in on Sundays, making the centre of the big cities look like a carnival as street vendors add to the melee. Families with more traditional values frown upon such activities.

Men will play chess, Chinese chess or cards for hours. Gambling is a national pastime and lottery ticket sellers are everywhere. Horseracing is legal and fights between Siamese fighting fish or crickets can be seen. Cockfighting remains the most popular form and the fowls may or may not be fitted with artificial spurs for the tussle.

Music and Dancing

The Vietnamese love music. Traditional music has been heavily influenced by the Chinese in the north, where a five-tone scale exists, and by the Khmers and Chams in the south, where they introduced a nine-tone scale. There has been a revival of interest in traditional music and performances are often staged by the music conservatories in Hanoi, Hue or in Ho Chi Minh City. A number of instruments are used and the five classic instruments are known as the five perfects. These constitute the *dan tam,* a three-stringed guitar, the *ty ba,* a pear-shaped, four-stringed guitar, the *nhi,* a two-stringed instrument similar to a violin that may be played across the knee, the *dan tranh,* a 16-stringed zither and the *kim,* similar to an elongated guitar. Some music is to be enjoyed on its own, other pieces accompany dances or opera and additional instruments are added as needed. Drums, a transverse bamboo flute called the *sao truc* and the *dan bau,* a monochord, single-stringed lute, are also seen.

The people's love of music can be seen in the fast expansion of karaoke, a modern blend of an old skill that is taking off among the wealthier city dwellers. While dancing was illegal from 1975 to 1986 it is now making a comeback and ballroom dancing is as popular as disco.

Theatre

Several types of traditional theatre exist. *Tuong* opera is a highly stylised, classic version with few stage props but very distinct painted faces. It came from central Vietnam and mostly depicts legends about superheroes. *Cheo* is popular opera from the north that is frequently humorous and involves singing and gesturing. *Cai Luong* from the south is known as "renovated" opera as it was introduced in the 1920s and combines French-style drama and singing and uses elaborate stage props. Another more unusual form is water puppetry, usually performed in a pond in villages. It dates back to ancient times and involves the villagers getting together to ask for the gods' blessings. Stories are from rural life or history and many reflect the strong sense of humour of the Vietnamese. This form was popular in the north and spread through the country during the Tran dynasty.

Sport

In the cities where people do not exert themselves physically working the land through the day, time is made for sport. Older people can be seen practising *tai chi* early in the morning or taking a walk. Young men take fitness seriously and many work out in gyms. Tennis is played by the wealthier people. Badminton, table tennis, soccer and volleyball are popular, as well as some lesser known games such as *da cau,* a children's game where something similar to a shuttlecock is kicked over a net. The game looks like a cross between soccer and volleyball. After school, children train in ballet, martial arts or music. Many join the Scouts or the Young Pioneers' Club, a government-run organisation.

Chapter Eight

BUSINESS ETIQUETTE

This chapter discusses some successful business techniques and some pitfalls to avoid, not all of which are purely cultural in derivation. The saying "When in Rome, do as the Romans do" is applicable to Vietnam too. Transplanting all aspects of a foreign work culture simply does not work. Some elements may but caution is advised. Several business people have been deported for using techniques here that they would have used back home. Others have offended influential people and been forced to leave.

Doing business in Vietnam can be time-consuming and often frustrating. One of the reasons for this is the bureaucracy that controls the system. A brief introduction to the government structure is essential if you are to understand any of the situations you may find yourself in, and this is outlined in the Resources chapter. Despite all this, conducting business can also be a surprisingly straightforward affair and while politeness and common sense are essential, Vietnam does not have as many subtleties and complexities of business as in, for instance, Japan and China.

If you are not joining an established business in Vietnam, do as much homework as possible before you arrive. The streets are not all paved with gold but are actually full of potholes for the unwary business person. Many fall victim and go home considerably poorer, with a very dim view of the country. All the investment rules and regulations should be carefully checked. They are literally changed on a daily basis, so make sure you get up-to-date information. Taxes can be quite high and the accuracy of most of the statistical information on the state of the economy and the market is questionable, to say the least. The Resources chapter outlines some of the business guides that are available now and there are many more in the pipeline.

How the Vietnamese View Foreigners

When Vietnam opened its doors to the outside world in the late 1980s, foreigners were welcomed as overseas experts who were able to improve the country's future. Recently, the reception has become more cautious as the Vietnamese have become accustomed to hearing promises of projects that do not eventuate or of ideas that benefit the foreign operator substantially more than the Vietnamese. Worse still, the Vietnamese experienced a series of foreign investment failures early on before they had developed the skills to differentiate good from bad projects. This has added to the general scepticism and mistrust of foreigners that must now be overcome.

Generally, foreign business people are still seen as a potential source of not just money, but also technology, education, the latest ideas and travel. Sometimes, this is gained directly as foreign companies employ locals or work in partnership with them. Or it may occur indirectly. Access to English lessons from native English speakers improves an individual's personal abilities to get a better job. On a broader scale, foreign companies bring internationalism which in turn creates wealth and, as the economy improves, a multiplier effect spreads the wealth to many levels.

For these reasons, among others, expectations are placed on the visitor. While you may be in Vietnam to achieve personal objectives and those of your company, the Vietnamese look upon your presence as something from which they should gain. Each foreigner is likely to find demands put on him—mostly to teach and pass on skills and knowledge. Long-term commitment to Vietnam is recognised and encouraged by the government so the pressures are felt at both individual and company levels. Provision of training courses for government staff, bursaries for university education and major renovations of important buildings (perhaps as your future office) are just a few of the possibilities.

The Basics

Start by brushing up on good personnel practices that can and should be applied anywhere in the world. On top of these, there are a few other considerations in Vietnam.

- Courtesy is very important. Always show respect for older people and those in positions of authority.
- Be honest and open in your approach. The Vietnamese will assess you and decide whether they can trust you and your company.
- Avoid showing anger or frustration. Some use it as part of a calculated ploy to help achieve their desired ends but it can create a situation that is hard to control.
- Do not cause someone to lose face in front of others. The people can and do hold a grudge for a long time and may get even with you somehow at a later stage. Even low-ranking staff can thwart your plans if they choose to do so.

OFFICIALS, PARTNERS AND BUREAUCRACY

Business Dealings Take Time

Various businesses have differing priorities and time scales. Whether you are a large multinational or a small entrepreneur, you will have to go through the bureaucracy of setting up. Someone must be in the country meeting the right people and gently pushing your claim. Always allow more time than you expect and do not think that giving a deadline will speed up the process. It will frequently be ignored. Your patience and eagerness to do business in Vietnam is being assessed at this stage, together with your commitment to your proposal and the financial backing you have. Plan for this or you will have to back out just weeks before a licence is to be issued, even if you have already laid the groundwork many months beforehand. Be patient. Go a little slower, rather than push ahead too fast, and you are more likely to succeed.

Money To Do Business

Although there is no minimum capital requirement for investment, Vietnam is not particularly interested in ventures with little capital behind them. Setting up is often expensive. Even researchers and aid agencies may be presented with hefty costs for expense items such as the hiring of cars. All foreigners are assumed to be wealthy and it will take time and persuasion to bring prices down to a reasonable level. You may have to come up with some face-saving ways to avoid expensive offers and find cheaper alternatives. You will also have to be careful not to cause the other party to lose face.

Dress Code

Appearance counts as it does in most other countries. The north is a little cooler and more formal than the south, so suits and ties are standard dress for men. In the south, jackets are less common as the weather is too hot but a short- or long-sleeved shirt in a conservative

Shoeshine services are available in the business districts, making dress standards a little easier to maintain.

colour, a tie and dark pants are commonly seen. For women, modest clothes covering the shoulders and knees are appropriate. If in doubt, veer towards the more formal and conservative. Clothes that are too casual show a lack of respect for the person you are meeting.

Starting Up

Who you know is crucial in Vietnam. Business is done through personal contacts and initially, you will need to work at finding and contacting the right people to help you. The importance of this stage cannot be underestimated and many businesses hit problem after problem because they have the wrong local partner or are getting poor advice.

There are several ways to approach this. Some of the big overseas accounting firms have offices in Vietnam and one of the many functions they perform is matching overseas investors with appropriate Vietnamese partners. Lawyers and banks can also provide this service but be clear about the kind of partner you want and why.

You may have your own contacts and choose to do things a different way, but double-check the credentials of your prospective partner or higher-ranking Vietnamese staff whom you may have to deal with. There is still a good deal of distrust and dislike for Viet Kieu (overseas Vietnamese), particularly within government circles. If you employ one, or have one as a partner, ensure that you also have a very good and well-connected Vietnamese adviser to help overcome any problems which may arise. Also think carefully about the politics of having a northerner or southerner as a partner. Like it or not, politics will play a large part in the success or failure of your business.

Meeting People

It cannot be overemphasised that all business is conducted through personal contact. This is true in many parts of the world but particularly so in Vietnam. There is no legal framework for commercial transactions as yet. If or when disputes arise, your personal contacts will be the only ones available to help settle them.

Find out who you should meet with and then get a third party to introduce you personally, or get a letter of introduction from a mutual friend or acquaintance. Not only is this the traditional way of doing business but if you approach the other party without a proper introduction, you may well not be taken very seriously. Too many foreigners have been known to arrive and make lots of promises that do not eventuate. The Vietnamese are not necessarily familiar with the names of foreign companies, no matter how well-established they may be overseas, and it is not easy for them to check your credentials.

It is possible to set up meetings without an introduction but expect to take an extra three to four meetings to reach the same stage as if you had been introduced. The first few times may be very difficult because of the scepticism towards foreigners but if you have the time, this is not necessarily a bad approach as it allows both sides to become more comfortable with each other and this can pay off in the long term.

Gain contacts with other foreign business people who may have had to face similar issues. Register at the embassy; make contact with your country's official business promoter (if there is one); attend social functions, sports clubs and running groups like the Hash House Harriers; and start meeting people. Not only will they provide important contacts and be able to advise on issues they have already had to tackle, but Vietnam is still a small place and keeping your ear close to the grapevine can give you a lot of additional information.

BUSINESS MEETINGS

Important meetings should always be held in the morning, if possible. Afternoons are usually reserved for dealing with more operational matters. Meetings take far longer than you may anticipate so do not try to fit too many into one day.

You are likely to be seated at a long, narrow table facing each other. The exchange of name cards is normal and one should be given to everyone present as, initially, you may not understand each person's role fully. Give the first one to the most senior person and deliver it with a handshake, using both hands if they are very senior. See Chapter 6, Communication for information on greetings and introductions.

It is impolite to rush the issue you want to speak about. Lengthy introductory speeches may be given. Patience is the main criterion. At initial discussions, one rarely gets straight to the point. Depending on your situation, it can take a least a dozen visits before you really get to know each other and more direct discussions can begin. This time of building trust is crucial. The real issues and concerns will appear with time. Instead of talking directly about establishing contracts, talk instead about the general economy and your business, what it involves and the approach you intend to take in Vietnam. Ask your business contacts about their company and use the discussion to gauge how far they have moved towards a profit-making centre as opposed to a socialist enterprise.

Even at later meetings, chat about your family and ask about theirs, the weather, the industry or recent events in Vietnam. Praise their country and the helpful people you have met. These and other topics should be discussed as you sip green tea, perhaps eat fruit and maybe smoke a cigarette as you get to know one another. This custom stems from the past when all discussions started with the chewing of betel nut before real subjects were discussed. Wait until the most senior person has had his first sip of tea before you touch yours.

In some areas, the people will be very upfront, almost brash with their answers, and you may be surprised at the directness of their questions and answers. But there are always areas they would rather not discuss, topics or information they do not wish you to know, and the truth or disclosure of these will only be revealed over time and numerous meetings.

Personal Assessments

Your initial talks with the Vietnamese will allow them to judge you and your company. Contracts may be signed and permission may be granted to proceed in various matters if they trust you. The Vietnamese value honesty and integrity. If they think you are being devious or are likely to let them down, you will never get past the first stage. Spend time to explain fully all the consequences of the proposal you are putting forward. Do not assume that everything has been communicated just because your proposal has been translated for them in writing. Spell out all the terms to minimise misunderstandings that can occur later. If the people think that you had hidden something from them earlier, you will find a brick wall placed before you. Also, use your initial meetings to explain things from your company's point of view so that they can understand your perspective and the things that are important to you.

Achieving Consensus

If you are to get approval from a company or government, many

191

people will have to agree that the proposition you are putting forward is a good one. There are no single decision-makers. Unfortunately, because of the maze of roles, positions and real power, you will never be 100% certain if you have identified all the major players correctly. Even a relatively low-ranking person may prove to be the stumbling block to achieving consensus although all the higher-ranking people agree to your proposal. So never ignore those in the lower positions.

When there are only one or two dissenters, you may be given an indication that you are close to achieving success. But you will never be told officially who the dissenters are or what the problem is (as this would cause them to lose face). But it is possible to find out informally and meet with these people over lunch or coffee to clear up the problem. They may raise a direct objection against your proposal or may simply want more time to assess your character and your business and decide how honest and trustworthy you are.

Sometimes, you will hit an impasse. One person may not agree—perhaps for no other reason than that he does not like the shape of your face (physiognomy) or does not trust foreigners. It is rare to be able to work around these people. You may simply have to start again elsewhere!

Arranging High-level Meetings

People are not prepared to commit themselves to a meeting many days in advance. Things are done at short notice and this may make things difficult for you when your bosses from overseas are coming to inspect your operations, explore new possibilities or meet business contacts and government officials. You can make a tentative appointment two to three weeks in advance, reconfirm a few days prior to it and telephone again 10 minutes before you leave to ensure that no higher party has usurped your meeting time. The better your personal relations with the people you are meeting, the more likely they are to honour the time slot you have been given. Make sure that your secretary is on good terms with their secretary. Allow her time to visit their office, deliver gifts on appropriate occasions and chat! If the meeting you have planned is a very important one for you, make sure that the message gets across.

If things go wrong and the person you would like to see is unavailable, you may not be told that he is in another meeting. His secretary will avoid the issue as it is embarrassing and you may just be left there cooling your heels! At other times, the second-in-command may join you instead if he is available.

Note-taking at Meetings

The Vietnamese rarely take notes. You may do so for your own purposes. The only meetings where minutes are always taken is at ministerial level and a copy will be sent to you soon afterwards.

PRESENTS TO OFFICIALS

There are occasions in business that may merit gifts. There is a narrow line between gift-giving and bribery or corruption. Most people and companies have strong rules to curb the latter, which are illegal in Vietnam. However, gifts are commonly given and are a regular part of doing business. There are no hard and fast rules about what to give but some general rules do apply. Chapter 7, Socialising in Vietnam outlines suitable gifts and some of the occasions when they should be sent. Presents brought back from overseas are always much appreciated. If you know your business associate's family background, it is also appropriate to bring back a small gift for his wife or child instead of one for him.

It is a good idea to have a Vietnamese counterpart advise you on the type of gift and the appropriate time to send it. He can deliver it for you as well. The secret is to give a present of the right value to the right person at the right time and, unless you have lived in Vietnam for a long period, you are likely to make mistakes!

Generally, as the status of the person increases, so should the value of the gift. Also, as your relationship strengthens and the person has done more favourable work for you, so should the value of their reward rise. Do not forget the bottom-ranking people. Remember that they can block or stall things. They may also be in line for promotions and the Vietnamese have good memories, so making friends now can pay off later. Small ways in which you can show someone some kindness and convey your thanks may be to offer him a cigarette or a ride in your car. Of course, the most cherished motivator a company can give is an overseas trip as part of a fact-finding mission or training course.

BUSINESS DINNERS

These may not occur after the first meeting but at a later stage, when relationships are more firmly established. Social occasions such as dinners are the time to talk about families and other areas of interest so that you get to know the people better and friendships can develop. Read Chapter 7, Socialising in Vietnam about hosting or being hosted by the Vietnamese and also Chapter 9, Eating Vietnamese Food for more information about Vietnamese food and how to eat it.

Often, your Vietnamese associates will choose the restaurant. Do not be surprised if it is one that serves unusual meats. Perhaps it is an offal dish, snake blood and meat, or even pangolin and other animals. The Vietnamese have a great sense of humour and the meal may be selected partly for its entertainment value as they watch your reactions and how you cope.

The success of your endeavours should be toasted before the meal. Extreme courtesy and formality is called for here and it is an ideal time to tell them how happy you are to be in Vietnam and how much you enjoy working with each of them.

Always have the speeches before the main meal is served as the dinner can progress two ways. Family affairs see everyone departing straight after the meal. People get up early both in the city and country and hence do not stay up late. Alternatively, the party may be a rowdy one and it can degenerate into a lot of drinking and no one will

Office parties are a good opportunity to get to know more about the people you work with.

remember what you had said earlier. It is polite to join in and applaud your own speech. Everyone waits until the person of highest authority leaves before taking their departure.

Carousing

Celebrations are held to mark special business events such as the granting of a lease, a business anniversary or the signing of a new contract. To mark the occasion, a dinner, speeches and toasts are in order. *Tram phan tram* is a drinking toast every visitor to the country hears at some stage. It means "100%" and each person at the table will toast you in this manner. Ten other people present means 10 drinks, each downed in one go. Several drinks later, the evening can become quite riotous, with empty bottles lined up or kicked under the table to show for it.

195

If you can stagger through it all, you will earn their respect and draw closer to them. But everyone has their own polite ways of avoiding getting hopelessly drunk, having a very late night with an adjournment to "girlie bars" and, perhaps, ending up with a large business expense to right off. Some speak to the most senior person in the group beforehand and get their help to escape an extended drinking session (too old; bad for the stomach, head, heart; doctor's orders and so on). Others "bargain" over the amount of drinks that they consume. You can have one round with everyone at the table instead of having to drink separately with each person. Ensure that it is beer and not whisky or, better still, if you really want to avoid alcohol, you can drink tea or soft drinks.

Women, especially, can ask for a soft drink and leave the party early. Older men will also find it easier to back out without losing the respect of the others in the group. The important part is drinking with your guests and establishing a bond, so at least drink something with them. However, it is not just foreigners who have to go through extended sessions of drinking and carousing and many Vietnamese business people have found ways to get around them. Country people are more used to drinking than business people in the city and you can expect a long, rough night on occasions.

TRANSLATOR ETIQUETTE

There are times when you will need to use a translator. Even if you speak a little Vietnamese or the other party speaks some English, it is more convenient and misunderstandings are minimised if a translator is present. Do not talk to the translator but turn to the person you are addressing and speak to him, using first-person pronouns. Regardless of the language barrier, nod and pay full attention to the person speaking, even though you may not understand the words. Let him speak uninterrupted and make notes about queries you wish to raise on certain points. This is far more polite than interrupting the speech.

Choose your translator carefully. Some people prefer to rotate the people they use so that the translator does not develop rapport with the other company and a commission is not built into the deal for them. Others take the opposite tack and use the same translator to develop a three-way rapport and cement business relationships.

SUPERSTITIONS

Some Vietnamese are very superstitious. You may not see or hear much about this except, perhaps, when it concerns the selection of auspicious dates for starting a business or undertaking a trip, event or celebration. These things may not affect your personal plans but should be taken into account when scheduling opening ceremonies, signing contracts or reaching major agreements with your Vietnamese counterparts, staff or customers who may subscribe to superstitious beliefs, no matter how modern they appear to be. Alternatively, you may wonder why the signing of a deal has been delayed for a few days. It is unlikely that you will get a direct answer but usually, it is because people are waiting for the right date to arrive.

Geomancy may affect a construction plan and physiognomy is used by some business people to determine who should be employed. Small altars may be placed in a room to keep the spirits happy.

CROSS-CULTURAL VARIATIONS

Many of the higher-ranking business people and government officials are well acquainted with international ways of doing business. They have lived and studied in Eastern European countries when Vietnam and the USSR maintained close ties. This can produce odd incidents where a person slips into Russian-style negotiating techniques (loud, direct speech and hammering the table with his fist during arguments) before reverting back to his more reserved Vietnamese ways.

BUSINESSWOMEN

Businesswomen have little trouble operating in the country and, in fact, often find it far more egalitarian than many Western countries as the Vietnamese are used to women working and holding positions of power. Occasional situations where a much younger expatriate female has difficulties supervising an older Vietnamese man occur but, generally, there is no problem delegating work, making decisions or giving orders. Life can be easier for you than your male counterparts as there is less pressure to go out drinking and partying until the early hours of the morning.

However, Vietnamese men tend to judge women by their own standards. Dress conservatively if you are single and be very discreet about boyfriends. Women who smoke and drink alcohol regularly are likely to be propositioned. Those who do not smoke or drink will be treated with courtesy and respect. Do not be offended if people make regular comments on your appearance. They are simply being polite and making conversation, even if it includes personal comments such as the growth of a pimple on your cheek.

YOUR OFFICE

You are likely to have office staff to deal with and, as you see these people every day, subtle cross-cultural differences become more obvious. As with all Vietnamese, you will earn their respect and win their loyalty as you settle in. This does not come easily, however. They will judge you in your first few weeks and it can be a very long, hard process to regain any credibility once you have lost it.

Business Hours

Normal Vietnamese office hours are not the same as those observed by most foreign companies, which are usually open from 8 a.m. to 5 p.m. The Vietnamese vary a little but usually start the day at 7–7.30 a.m., take a one-and-a-half to two-hour lunch break and finish by 4.30 pm. Because so many people hold at least two jobs to earn extra money, you will often find your staff leaving well before 4.30 p.m.

Lunch is followed by a siesta and most shops or businesses that remain open over lunch will have someone sleeping in them. Spell out your office hours clearly. Make it known to the staff that you expect them to arrive on time and that they should not leave early. Also state whether or not they can sleep in the office over the lunch break. If you allow this, discuss who should answer the telephone or look after the front counter. The staff can work out a rotation of duties among themselves but if it is not specifically mentioned, they will probably all go for lunch at once and leave the office unattended.

Hiring Staff

As in all other countries, there are good and poor performers in the work place. Here, the process can be complicated as many business establishments do not hire direct, but through a service company. Therefore, firing a person may not halt his salary (as it comes from the service company, not you). So the threat of firing is not a motivator. It can also be extremely difficult to do so without causing long-term problems, so it is important to hire the right people.

Consider not only a person's skills, but where he is from. Northerners and southerners do not necessarily get along. A northerner hired by a southern firm started and lasted three days. The new employee left voluntarily after being ostracised by her fellow workers. The boss suffered a deluge of complaints, based on nothing more than the new person's origins. They did not trust her. She was different, even though they already had a northerner working with them. He was accepted as he had already lived in the south for some time. Despite this example, most companies have a mixture of staff. There are generally few problems and benefits can result if you have to do business with both the north and south.

Micro-management

All foreigners in Vietnam have commented, at one point or another, that they had underestimated the amount of time and energy they had to spend to get their businesses going. Part of the problem is trying to slalom through a slow-moving bureaucracy. The other issue is training staff to run the business the way you want it. One business-man described Vietnam as "the land of children" and while that may be unfair, there is some truth in it when it comes to supervising office staff. Not only is very close supervision necessary, but most staff seem to prefer it.

Training

Few of your office staff would have had much experience dealing with the latest technology and foreign management styles. Added to this is the problem of communication. This places a heavy burden on you to conduct ongoing training. You will have to show your staff how things are to be done—from filing, correct formatting of a letter and speaking to a client in a polite business manner to the process of checking that all copies of a photocopying job are there. And these do not even touch on the technical aspects of your business! Evenings are often spent doing the normal work that you should have done during the day. The good thing about it all is that the Vietnamese are quite open to ideas and assimilate new concepts readily.

Taking the Initiative

Freedom to show initiative and take responsibility for decisions is not something that the Vietnamese have been brought up with, so most are not yet comfortable with the idea. While procedural training can be quite fast, it is much more difficult to encourage them to show initiative. There is a fear of risk-taking. Decisions are made by consensus. Most are not put into writing as it would mean that someone has to sign at the bottom of the page. Recent history has made the Vietnamese very wary of sticking their neck out and it can be very difficult to break this habit even within the narrow confines of work.

Learning from Mistakes

Mistakes need to be handled carefully. To point one out and raise the problems that it has caused can be too confrontational. Traditionally, mistakes are ignored, avoided and never addressed directly. Mistakes that have to be fixed or corrected will be rectified quietly, without an apology, so no one suffers a loss of face. This idea is compounded by a natural unwillingness to own up as the person will be held account-able. In local companies, the cost of errors is often taken out of a person's salary, even if it is a large amount. A bus driver was taking a new imported tourist bus from Hue to Da Nang and a stone flew up and chipped the windscreen. The cost of importing a replacement windscreen came to several months' salary and the amount was deducted from the driver's pay over a period of time.

If you are supervising staff, you will need to nurture an atmos-phere in which mistakes can be observed and used as a training tool so that they are not repeated. This can be done obtusely by noting problems that arise and, in a staff meeting, allowing the members to solve the problem without names being mentioned.

Delegation

Be very clear about the delegation of tasks. The Vietnamese tend to do exactly as they have been told and no more. Make it clear who is to do what in the office to avoid one person re-delegating the task to another person (often from a man to a subordinate woman). The flip side of the coin can also occur and a young Vietnamese graduate may have trouble delegating work to an older, established secretary. Avoid these issues by encouraging a team environment, not line control.

A Team Environment

The Vietnamese tend to have quite a dictatorial style of supervision but most foreigners find that promoting a team environment works best. It certainly fits far better into the Vietnamese psyche than promoting competition between individuals. Fellow workmates are like an extension of the family. Productivity can be improved by appealing to this sense and regular team meetings are one of the smoothest ways of resolving issues and problems that occur in the workplace. For instance, instead of telling off a person who was supposed to have answered telephone calls over lunch yesterday but did not, the issue can be raised at a staff meeting or written on the "problems board". Everyone will know who you are referring to even though names are not mentioned. In this way, no one loses face.

Observing Seniority

Age is very important to the Vietnamese and an early question will often be "How old are you?" The answer determines both the form of address they will use and their behaviour. They find it difficult to guess the ages of foreigners and even a couple of years' difference between people changes the pecking order. In work situations, seniority in position usually comes with age and experience. The Vietnamese expect foreigners to observe these rules and can be quite flustered if a young expatriate does not give an older colleague the respect that they believe should be forthcoming. The young person automatically loses the respect of the others.

These days, the correct forms of address can get quite confusing. A young, capable, well-educated foreigner may be placed in a more senior business position than an older Vietnamese. The younger person should respectfully listen to the older person's point of view until he has, at least, had the chance to earn some credibility in the office. Even if an older person joins a new company in a high position, he should be quite respectful towards lower-ranking staff until he has demonstrated his skills and won the respect of the others within the organisation. This also holds true for Vietnamese dealing with each other in the workplace. For one thing, they know to use the correct pronoun in addressing each other to convey the respect intended.

Time

Time is treated a little oddly. People are quite punctual and if you are late for a meeting, they may tell you so. However, the time it takes to do a task may be seen as immaterial. "Patience is a virtue" is a saying that could have been written specifically with the Vietnamese in mind. Efficiency and quick decisions are not necessarily important to them. It can be very frustrating to try and get things done quickly. Sometimes, things are held up by bureaucracy but there is not always an obvious reason. Learn to be patient and provide for extra time— you will certainly need it. When dates or timing becomes a critical issue, explain why. Spell out the bigger picture from your perspective because the people are unable to see it on their own. Hire a translator if necessary to make sure that there are no misunderstandings.

Financial Control

As staff training starts to pay off, the burden does get lighter but it is also time to put checks in place. The Vietnamese are used to having cuts on all financial dealings. Whoever hires the office vehicle will receive a kickback from the car hire company. This is also the case with the hotel you use, the factory you choose to do business with and the stationery company you patronise. There are many ways to tackle this but if you choose to ignore it, what starts as a trickle of money going out soon turns into a flood, decreasing profits significantly as everyone boosts their salary at your company's expense. Some business people pay a portion of staff salaries on a commission basis, turning one set of kickbacks into a formalised process. Others simply have to check all accounts carefully and plug each hole as it is noticed. How you do it will depend on the type of business you are in and your personal management style. Whatever your technique, you will have plenty of practice refining it.

Clamping Down

There will be times when it is appropriate to reprimand staff. Always plan this in advance and try not to fly off the handle. Causing someone to lose face is one of the most serious offences you can commit. History has some lessons in this area. During the Vietnam War, the

Viet Minh found that psychological methods of reprimand were far more effective than physical beatings. Public criticism is very severe so do not castigate a staff member in front of others.

Alternatively, you can take the heat away from yourself by getting your overseas boss (if you have one) to pinpoint a problem. You receive a directive from him asking for an issue to be investigated. Have an office policy written down covering leave, clothing allowances and other issues. This stops staff accusing you of favouritism, even if it is not present.

Staff Motivators

Imported gifts are highly valued and the types of presents and the times that they may be given are outlined in Chapter 7, Socialising in Vietnam. Additional motivators or rewards to hardworking staff can be as varied. Some people take their staff out for lunch or dinner and may include their families as well. This helps to create a bond and promote loyalty. It may also be done to celebrate birthdays, depending on how many staff you have working for you. Small offices have been known to organise a day trip to the beach for staff and their families (from Ho Chi Minh City to Vung Tau, for instance) or to allow an extra day off as a reward. Personal boosts can be given to staff not just through gifts or wage increases; the most popular method is to send them overseas on a business or training trip.

Staff bonuses are also paid at Tet, but these are considered mandatory rather than a reward. Some companies, mostly the Vietnamese ones, give bonuses on National Day but this is not essential. Using festival or holiday bonuses or gifts as a reward for a selected few may cause resentment among the others. Salary rises or performance reviews will be compared. You may try to give these out privately but expect each of your staff to know exactly what was said and how much money was received by each of the other staff members. Someone will almost certainly come back to you demanding to know the reason for the differences.

LETTERS

Formal letters typed on letterhead are the most common way in which people write to each other. It is worth remembering that a personal letter in your own handwriting carries a great deal more weight. It shows the value that you place on the subject and the person you are writing to. It is rarely used in business but may be employed for a letter of introduction, for instance.

STORY TELLERS

The Vietnamese love to tell tales on each other. Once the initial barriers have been broken, you will start to hear gossip and stories of what another staff member has or has not done. This can be useful and some managers cultivate it as a technique for keeping track of people and happenings in the office. They can stop problems in the early stages, thanks to the grapevine. Others choose to ignore it and make it known that they are not interested, as it can be petty and time-consuming.

ABSOLUTE DON'TS

The Vietnamese are a very proud people no matter what their job. Colonialist attitudes will lose you respect faster than anything else. One example is cutting back on items for local staff but allowing the same or more expensive items for foreign staff without giving good reasons. It is considered a direct put-down of Vietnam and its people if you tell your staff they are lucky to work for a foreign company because it offers higher pay, or that they should pull their socks up as there are many other people wanting a well-paid job like theirs. You will lose their respect and loyalty for displaying such an attitude towards them.

— Chapter Nine —

EATING VIETNAMESE FOOD

Vietnamese food is excellent and appeals to most people. While it is not as well-known as Chinese or Thai food, it is a distinct and refined cuisine in its own right. Flavours, textures, cooking techniques and even ingredients have all been introduced into Vietnamese cuisine over time, but it still retains its own unique character. A southern dish may have many of the same ingredients as a Thai one: garlic, fish sauce, shrimp paste, coriander, basil, lemon grass, mint and chilli. But the Vietnamese dish will not have the overpowering spicy character and strength of the Thai dish. It will be more subtle and less hot. The Vietnamese spring roll (called *cha gio* in the south and *nem sai gon*

or *nem ran* in the north) may sound in name like the Chinese ones but it is smaller and crispier. The filling, the outside wrapping and the way it is eaten are all different from its Chinese counterpart.

Vietnamese food can be characterised by the way it combines complementary ingredients and contrasting textures. Texture variation is as important as the final flavour. Crunchy, roasted peanuts often top a soft noodle dish and crisp fried shallots, known as *hanh kho phi,* will be sprinkled over a dish.

Cooking techniques are similar to Chinese ones but the preferred style varies throughout the regions. To stir-fry, a cook uses long bamboo chopsticks, not a stirrer or frying ladle, as the Chinese do.

Vietnamese food is also very healthy. A stir-fry dish will use much less oil than a Chinese equivalent. A light vegetable oil is used in preference to lard. Thickened sauces are unusual, so the food is well suited to diet-conscious foreigners. Salads are often a combination of meat or seafood and vegetables like *ga xe phai* or shredded cabbage. A wide variety of ingredients is used in a salad to ensure that there is a good contrast in colour, texture and taste. It makes an excellent light lunch or dinner but is rarely eaten on its own by the Vietnamese. They prefer to share a number of dishes by placing them in the centre of the table and allowing guests to help themselves so that a greater variety of food is available to all.

HISTORICAL DEVELOPMENT

Vietnam's geographic location has given it some wonderful advantages when it comes to eating. Stretching as it does from the subtropical southern parts, through mountainous plateaus and coastal plains, to the much cooler northern region, virtually all foods can be grown somewhere in the country. Rice is predominant in the flat river plains while cashews, durians, breadfruits, limes and many vegetables grow well in the south. From the cooler hills of Da Lat, strawberries, grapes, potatoes and tomatoes keep Ho Chi Minh City well supplied. Further north, cherries, apples, wheat and other crops flourish.

The country's food has developed along with its culture over the past 1,000 years. History has had its impact on the kitchen too and culinary influences from China, Mongolia, Thailand, Indonesia and, more recently, France and the United States, have all changed eating habits in Vietnam. Aspects of each of these have been assimilated into the native character of Vietnamese cooking but none has dominated it completely. New ingredients, different cooking techniques as well as whole dishes have been adopted.

The Chinese influence on Vietnamese cuisine is the strongest by far and this is not surprising, considering 10 centuries of domination. The Chinese introduced stir-frying, deep-frying in a wok and eating with chopsticks. Perhaps one of the greatest culinary changes came with the introduction of Buddhism, which is now very strong throughout the country. Monks and nuns do not eat meat and followers abstain from it regularly. This has led to a wonderfully varied vegetarian diet, although meat dishes are also popular.

Mongolian invasions into northern Vietnam in the 10th century directly added beef dishes such as *pho bo* (a beef and noodle soup) and *bo bay mon* (beef cooked seven ways) to the menu. They remain distinctly northern dishes but are popular throughout the country. In the south, the influences of Cambodia, Laos and Thailand are much stronger and from these countries came some Indian influences. For instance, Saigon soup, *hu tieu,* uses flat Cambodian-style egg noodles instead of rice noodles. The use of spices and chilli is much more widespread and curries using coconut milk can be found.

From the 16th century onwards, as explorers came and later settled, new food items were introduced. From the New World came watercress, corn, potatoes and tomatoes. Snow peas were introduced by the Dutch and became known as "Holland peas" while the French brought asparagus or "Western bamboo shoots".

The French influence is strong due to the country's colonial domination for nearly a century. Vendors with fresh baguettes, baked twice a day, sit at street corners. These rolls are sliced open and a mixture of salad, locally made paté and pork fat is put inside to make a quick meal. *Café au lait* is still one of the most popular drinks, even if the milk used is almost always sweetened condensed milk. Yogurt is a regular snack and milk, butter, custard tarts, pastries and cakes have all become a part of Vietnamese life. In the south, the French method of sautéing in a frying-pan is preferred to the Chinese style of stir-frying in a wok. Prepared desserts are not traditionally eaten but crème caramel, or a Vietnamese version made from coconut milk, is commonly seen on menus.

Regional foods show the emigration of certain ethnic groups from China into Vietnam. The Hakka people, together with many Cantonese, moved southwards in the 17th century and settled in northern Vietnam, bringing dishes such as *dau phu nhoi* or stuffed beancurd, an adaptation of a Hakka dish. In Cholon, the Chinese quarters of Ho Chi Minh City, dishes adapted from the Chinese are enjoyed. These include *mi vit tie,* or egg noodle soup with braised duck.

INGREDIENTS

Many of the ingredients are well-known in Asian cooking. Bamboo shoots, *tofu* or beancurd, Chinese cabbage, bean sprouts and Chinese kale are used widely. Shallots, particularly flowering chives, are used in abundance. Eating lotus seeds or the stem ensures that you will have a good night's sleep, according to local belief, and both are found in many dishes. In contrast, the widespread use of MSG, or monosodium glutamate, may cause you to stay awake (see the Stay Healthy section in Chapter 5, Culture Shock).

Water spinach, *rau muong,* is probably the most widely used vegetable in Vietnam. Because northerners eat so much of it, they have a saying that when they travel, it follows them around like a tail. It is favoured, not only because it grows quickly and easily, but also because it provides an ideal contrast of textures once it is cooked. The leaves go limp while the stems remain firm and crunchy. For similar reasons, bean sprouts is one of the favourite vegetables of the

Fresh food is emphasised in Vietnamese cooking.

southerners. Such is the emphasis on texture that cooks use alum, which helps to keep food crunchy.

Noodles are an ingredient that is rarely made at home. Instead, specialists prepare them and sell them daily, wrapped in a banana leaf. Similarly, paté is enjoyed by many but the tedious process of grinding the meat until it is smooth means that it is not produced at home. Instead, commercial paté makers with large machines provide a ready supply to the markets.

Because of Vietnam's long coastline, seafoods have always been a major source of protein. Freshwater and saltwater species are common and the emphasis is always on freshness, as no refrigeration is available in most places. Crab, shrimp, cuttlefish, clams, eel, shellfish and many species of fish can be bought. Meats vary in quality. Beef tends to be expensive as there is not much suitable land for cattle to graze. It can be tough but usually has a good flavour. Chicken and duck are free range, juicy with great flavour, but not sc tender. Pork is one of the favourite meats. Everywhere, the quality is good and the price cheap but the pork from Hue is said to be the best. Supposedly, it is a smaller beast fed on rice and the trunk of the banana tree, both of which contribute to its superior flavour. Frogs' legs are good but lamb and mutton are rarely seen.

Nuoc Mam

While many of the ingredients are not unique to Vietnam, the one ingredient that is quintessentially Vietnamese is the distinctive fish sauce, *nuoc mam*. It is not the same as fish sauces made in other countries and lends a distinct dimension to Vietnamese food.

Nuoc mam comes from the liquid drained from salted, fermented fish. It is used in virtually every dish in much the same way that soy sauce is used in Chinese food. Often, it appears as a dipping sauce, taking the place of salt on a Western table. Or it can be mixed with garlic, chilli, sugar, vinegar and fresh lime to make *nuoc cham*. Every cook varies the ingredients a little to achieve the right blend.

Right along the length of Vietnam's coastline, people brew *nuoc mam*. Different combinations of fish species and a few secret ingredients help to add colour and flavour and result in many different blends. The fish are alternately layered with salt and left in huge wooden barrels (concrete tanks are more commonly used these days) for three months. The liquid is removed from the base via a tap and poured back into the top and left for another three months. The brew is then ready for sale, or it can be aged further. The flavour improves over the years, making aged *nuoc mam* like fine wine to a connoisseur.

The islands of Phu Quoc produce a wonderful brew noted for its clarity and flavour. The best grade is from the first draining, as with olive oil. It is usually very dark in colour, very viscous and expensive, with the label marked *nhi* or *thuong hang* indicating that it is of the highest quality. A cheaper grade of *nuoc mam* is made after the first grade has been drained off. Fresh water is added to the mixture and, after pressing, a clear, lighter liquid is drained off. This *nuoc mam* is used in cooking. Newcomers to Vietnam often find the initial smell of the sauce a little offensive, but it tends to blend with other ingredients and highlight their flavours rather than override them. Hotels catering for tourists will not always serve it, fearing that foreigners will not like it. However, it is a must if you want to savour authentic Vietnamese food.

Rice

Rice is the symbol of life. It is called the pearl of the gods and is an integral part of any meal. Its importance is reflected in the number of words in the Vietnamese language describing it at every stage of its growth and journey, from rice seed to the table. Children who do not finish all the rice in their bowl at meal time may be told by their mothers that, in their next life, they will always be hungry. There are literally dozens of varieties of rice, each varying a little in flavour, colour, amount of gluten, texture and aroma. Many Vietnamese can differentiate between the types of rice and identify each by the aroma it gives off after it is cooked. People who cannot afford the more expensive, aromatic varieties will add a few *la dua* leaves to improve the scent. For the Westerner, shopping for rice can be bewildering. Good Vietnamese cooks tend to buy their rice from a regular rice dealer whose advice they trust. The quality and price will be debated at length while the customer is treated courteously and served tea and candies as they talk.

Different rice types are used for different purposes but generally, a long-grain, white rice that remains dry and flaky after cooking is preferred for steaming. The best grains will be soft but not soggy when cooked and they tend to be long and narrow with pointed ends. Hue is known for producing *com huong giang,* a spicy, fragrant and tasty variety of rice. Shorter, rounder varieties may harden when cooked and left to cool, and are not preferred. Vegetarians tend to use a lot of glutinous rice and combine it with legumes and nuts as it is more nutritious.

Rice is used for much more than just boiling. Rice paper, *banh trang,* is a round, brittle sheet made from rice flour, salt and water. It is often laid out on bamboo mats and placed along road kerbs to allow it to dry in the sun. This gives the rice paper its attractive, crosshatched design. It is used as the outer wrapper in Vietnamese spring rolls. It is also used uncooked for wrapping other types of food and is much crispier and smaller than the Chinese equivalent. Triangular-shaped rice papers are used to wrap cooked food at the table.

Rice also can be made into various noodles. Rice sticks or *banh pho* are used mainly in stir-fried dishes or in soups. Very thin rice vermicelli, *bun* or *banh hoi,* is popular in soups and salads and can be served cold as an accompaniment to curries or grilled meats.

A roasted rice powder, *thinh,* is used as flavouring. Rice vinegar has a milder, sweeter taste than white vinegar. Rice is even used to make a sweet rice wine, *de,* produced from mixing cooked glutinous rice with yeast, sugar and a little flour, then letting the mixture ferment. Rice wine is drunk extensively in the country after a day's work, or consumed at lunch by men. City folk look upon it as the drink of manual workers. Often, only one small glass is used and is passed around among members of a group. Wealthier people drink beer.

FRUITS

A marvellous variety and supply of fruits are available. Some are native to the country, such as the strong-smelling durian. People either love or hate it but it should never be consumed with alcohol (the combination has killed people). While its strong, cloying smell is too much for many people, the flavour is not as strong and can be described as a cross between custard and onions. Watermelon, melon, pineapple, banana, litchi, papaya, rambutan, jackfruit, mangosteen and various citrus fruits are grown in Vietnam. Introduced species such as strawberries, pears and apples are favoured too. The green dragon fruit, grown on a weeping cactus, has an unusual skin which is shocking pink. Inside, the white flesh is full of tiny black seeds.

REGIONAL DIFFERENCES

Barbecued dishes, fish, seafood and fresh uncooked vegetables are enjoyed throughout Vietnam but regional variations, while not as distinct as in China, are still interesting to note as you travel around. Some of these are due to the climatic and geographical differences and, hence, the varying availability of ingredients. But some dishes are preferred in hotter or cooler areas, or tastes may have altered as an area comes under the influence of other countries. Certain regional dishes are now favourites throughout the country.

In the north, the influence of Chinese food is naturally stronger. Stir-fried food, congees, stews and soups are all popular. Few spices are used although black pepper is a popular condiment. Crab is included on the menu, but little fish is eaten regularly. Beef is more common. Hanoi's most famous food is probably *pho bo*. Boiling beef stock is poured over fresh rice noodles and wafer-thin slices of raw beef. Next, onion, green chilli peppers, lemon juice, coriander and mint are usually added. It is a popular dish consumed with great relish and makes for a hearty breakfast, lunch or dinner throughout the country. Some restaurants specialise in this dish and *pho* signs are a regular sight.

Winter in the north is cold and families gather around a big bowl of seasoned broth and cook vegetables and meat in it, as in a steamboat dish. *Cha ca,* a fish dish, is cooked this way and a charcoal brazier sits on the table to keep the broth boiling. The fire from the brazier spreads its warmth to the diners as well.

Well-decorated, sophisticated, multiple-dish meals characterise the food of Hue. Its chefs are said to be able to cook over 2,000 dishes as every meal for the king had to consist of 50 dishes. The royal capital dominated central Vietnam in the 19th century and its food reflects its former status. In the north or south, food is placed on the table with one large bowl containing each dish. In Hue, the same food is presented in many small bowls so that the table looks like a king's spread. Service is also very much more formal. Pork sausages known as *nems,* wonderfully flavoured vermicelli soups and sweet or salty rice cakes are renowned in this area. Vegetables such as potatoes, tomatoes, asparagus, artichokes and cauliflowers are grown locally and widely used. The people eat small cakes like *banh tom chay* and use dried chilli in their cooking.

A special shrimp sauce known as *mam tom* or *mam ruoc* is made in this region and characterises a lot of the dishes. The method of preparation is similar to that for *nuoc mam* but shrimps are used instead of fish. The shrimp sauce is used as a dip. It is very pungent and even many Vietnamese find the smell too strong for them!

The southern region of Vietnam grows a large variety of tropical and temperate fruits and vegetables but favours spicy dishes. Curries show the Indian influence. These may be served with noodles for a party, with rice as a family dish or with crunchy French bread as a light meal. *Thit kho nuoc dua,* or pork simmered in coconut milk, shows the southern influence and *banh xeo,* a thin pancake, is popular. Sugarcane and locally made sugar is used more widely than in the north. A popular dish is *cha tom,* or shrimp wrapped around sugarcane. Fruits like pineapple may be used as a fruit, or may take the place of a vegetable in a cooked dish. Cooking times tend to be shorter, and stews and deep-fried dishes are less common than in the north.

Dishes are often served in a way that is different from the south. Guests will have grilled food presented to them with a plate of fresh lettuce and herbs. Each person places a little of the cooked food in the centre of a lettuce leaf, adds the herbs according to their own preference, wraps the lettuce around the food and then dips it into a hot sauce. A vegetable platter will often have raw vegetables as well as unripe fruits such as mango, banana, papaya, starfruit or apple.

MEALS AND MEAL TIMES

The Vietnamese eat three meals a day. Breakfast is usually eaten between 6 and 7 a.m. It may consist of a sticky rice called *xoi,* a rice gruel called *chao,* congee served with seafood or meat, or a noodle soup such as *pho* or *chao canh.* The latter is a rice noodle soup with pork or chicken. French baguettes are baked early and these are filled with Vietnamese sausage, salad, onions, spicy sauce and pork fat, providing for a quick meal on the way to work.

Because people start the day early, lunch often begins around 11–11.30 a.m. Workers traditionally go home to eat with their families but in the cities, many remain in the office or eat at a nearby street cafe. Some pack food from home or buy it from a street vendor. The meal may comprise noodle soup, or barbecued meats and some pickled vegetables eaten with rice.

Dinner is the time when the family eats together. The meal is roughly of the same proportion and composition as lunch, comprising three parts—a soup with vegetables and a little meat in it, a protein dish of fish, meat or eggs, and rice. Wealthier families will have additional dishes to complement these. These foods are served simultaneously. Rice is first placed in the eating bowl. Morsels of different dishes will be dipped into a sauce and eaten with the rice. At the end of the meal, any remaining soup is poured over the rice in the bowl and eaten.

Dessert is rarely eaten after a meal although fresh fruit may be served. At restaurants, a small range of sweet foods can be enjoyed, some of French origin. The Americans have left a firm love for *kem,* or ice-cream, and several *kem* factories are doing well.

Sweet items and fruits are often eaten as snacks. These may be served with tea when a visitor comes, or after the lunchtime siesta as a pick-me-up. Bakery delights like *banh me,* or sesame cookies, are light but have a good flavour. Fried bananas, sweet potatoes and candied fruits like coconut, winter melon or lotus seeds provide quick snacks. The rainbow drink, *che hot sen that tranh,* a mixture of lotus seeds, iced jelly and mung beans, cools people down on a hot day. A sweet soup like *che chuoi,* or bananas in coconut milk, is another late afternoon snack, as is frozen, sweet yogurt.

THE ETIQUETTE OF EATING

Diners will usually sit around a table with a bowl sitting on a small plate, chopsticks and a soup spoon placed in front of each person. The small plate can be used for discarded bones, shrimp shells and so on. Chopsticks for daily use are normally made of plastic, bamboo or painted wood. Special occasions may see ebony or ivory chopsticks being used. They should be placed on the right of the bowl and on top of a napkin (if one is supplied). Chopstick rests are optional in Vietnam. The soup spoon, which should be placed on the left of the bowl, is usually plastic, ceramic or made of a metal such as stainless steel.

There will be at least one small dipping bowl at the top right hand side of the bowl for the *nuoc mam*, *nuoc cham* or other dipping sauces, depending on the complexity of the meal. A mixture of salt and pepper is often presented in a tiny bowl with a piece of fresh lime. You may want to squeeze the lime into the salt and pepper mixture. Chilli may be provided as another side dish.

Family eating etiquette varies through the regions. In the north and central areas, the oldest man will sit nearest the door and everyone else is arranged in descending order according to age. The oldest man starts first by putting food in his eating bowl. Before younger members start eating, they will request permission from each of the older members. As a guest, let the host or oldest person sit first. You will then be shown where to sit, usually directly opposite the host. The host will often take morsels of food from each dish and place them in your bowl. Eat only a little. Check if the others are also eating food from all the dishes. If they are only eating rice, stop and say you are full even if you are starving, as the family may not really have sufficient food for a guest. You can serve a little of the other dishes to another family member to show your thoughtfulness towards them.

Southerners will let you help yourself to as much or as little as you like from the central food bowls. Because they do not serve their guest directly, they are seen as more casual and impolite by northerners.

When taking food from the central food bowl, it should be done with a serving spoon so that you do not dip your chopsticks into it, thus "contaminating" the food. The bowl you eat from can be picked up with one hand and brought closer to the mouth, ensuring that more food can be consumed in a faster, tidier way.

The Vietnamese are noisy eaters and slurping noises are not considered impolite. When you pause between eating, place the chopsticks across your food bowl, or use the chopstick rest if this is provided. Do not stick them into your food bowl. Not only is it impolite, the chopsticks are also likely to tip out, spilling your food all over the table. Soup is often eaten last to clean out the rice bowl, but this is not a hard and fast rule. Good etiquette demands that you should not leave rice in your own bowl at the end of a meal. Not only is it a waste of resources, it is also inconsiderate of the effort that has gone into its production and preparation.

Dishes of crab or shrimp may require the use of fingers to shell them, in which case a finger bowl may be placed near you. It will contain lemon and either tea or water. Wash your fingers in the solution as it will help to get rid of grease and any strong smell.

There are a number of dishes that you may not like or may not want to try. In a restaurant, if you do not like a certain dish, indicate to the waiter that you do not want any of it—or to your host if he is serving from a central bowl or platter. If it has already been put into your bowl, it is polite to take a small bite of it rather than leave it untouched.

BEVERAGES

Tea, called *che or tra*, is the most common drink. It is drunk at any time during the day. Early each morning, a pot of tea is prepared and then kept warm with a padded cosy or in a thermos flask, to be drunk throughout the day. Any visitor is always served tea in tiny tea cups. It may still be warm from the time it was brewed. If not, a small amount is poured into a cup and hot water is added.

Green tea is made from leaves that are roasted immediately after they have been picked and is unfermented. Black tea is made from partially dried leaves that are fermented before they are fully dried. Many other types of tea also exist. Artichoke tea is made from boiling the dried vegetable. Dried flowers such as chrysanthemum, jasmine, lotus, hibiscus and rose may be added to tea to give it a special flavour and aroma.

Coffee is a popular legacy from French times. Most men drink it at breakfast and throughout the day although the women tend not to. It is strong and served filtered into individual glasses. It can be drunk straight or with milk. Milk is usually sweetened condensed milk or powdered milk, although fresh and ultra heat-treated (UHT) are becoming more commonly available. Iced French coffee, or *ca-phe sua da,* is popular.

Soft drinks such as Coca-Cola and Pepsi are becoming more common in the shops but do not ask for them at someone's home unless the drinks are offered to you. Soda, or *nuoc ngot,* can be drunk straight. It can also be made into soda *chanh* by adding lime juice, or soda *sua hot ga,* a rich drink, by adding sweet milk and egg yolk. A number of brands of mineral water, or *nuoc suoi* are also available. They may be produced locally or imported. Street vendors sell sugarcane juice, freshly squeezed with the help of a roller machine, or coconut water from fresh, young coconuts.

Alcohol is also served often. There are local beers such as 333, Huda, Saigon Beer and Halida, as well as international brands such as Carlsburg, Heineken, Tiger or San Miguel, which are now brewed in Vietnam. Imported alcohol such as whisky or brandy may be ordered for special occasions such as weddings or company functions. *Ruou* means wine in Vietnamese but the word is also used to describe alcohol made from any ingredient. Glutinous rice is used to make a fiery, clear liquid called *ruou de* or *choum*. It is similar to Japanese *sake* or Chinese *kao liang* and can be served warm and used for toasting during occasions such as weddings.

FESTIVE FOODS

Festivals and holidays, as well as weddings and other family celebrations, are always special occasions to the Vietnamese and banquets
are often held to celebrate. Many times, specific foods will be served
that may not be eaten at other times of the year. *Cha gio*—fried spring
rolls that are known as *nem sai gon* or *nem ran* in the north—are time-
consuming to prepare so they are made for special occasions only and
usually eaten at restaurants. So is *bo bay mon,* or beef cooked in seven
ways.

Party food is much more elaborate than daily family dishes, both
in the complexity of the recipe and the appearance and display of the
food. Several more dishes are prepared than on normal days. The
amount of time and preparation that go into them reflect the importance of the occasion or the stature of the guests. For instance, rice is
rarely served steamed or plain, but is cooked with extra ingredients to
enhance its flavour and colour. Soups will be more elaborate and will
not be served over the rice, as in a family meal.

More expensive foods are used. Steamed whole fish is common
and is often beautifully presented. For instance, it may be covered
with a fishing net carved out of a single piece of carrot providing
important variations in colour and texture. The head is considered a
delicacy and good luck will befall the person who eats it. Game birds
like pigeon and quail are usually seen only at ceremonies and
functions. They are often roasted and served in pieces to be dipped in
salt, pepper and *nuoc cham,* and washed down with icy beer. Duck is
also served on special occasions and may be cooked in a way similar
to the Chinese Peking Duck, but served in a very Vietnamese manner.
The crispy skin is left on and sliced pieces of the bird, together with
some rice vermicelli, are wrapped in a lettuce leaf and dipped in *nuoc
cham* before being consumed.

The structure of a festive meal alters as well. It is more likely that
the food will be spread out over several courses rather than be served
all at once. Appetisers will be supplied with drinks before the main

meal begins, after which soup, main dishes and an elaborately decorated rice dish will be placed on the table, course by course. Tea may be served before and after the meal but never during it. Vietnamese men enjoy alcohol with a meal; women usually take soft drinks.

Tet, or Vietnamese New Year, is the most important celebration in the calendar and *banh chung,* or New Year's rice cake, is eaten then. It is a mixture of glutinous rice filled with pork and mung beans and then wrapped in banana leaves and steamed. It will be served with *dua mon,* which is vegetables in fish sauce. The story of its invention reveals something about the Vietnamese. A king in ancient Vietnam had many wives and children. When the time came to choose his successor, he called them together and announced that the child who could prepare the dish with the best symbolic meaning would become king. The children then scattered far and wide throughout the land searching for exotic and rare ingredients, except for the youngest son, who prayed day and night for heavenly inspiration. One night, as he slept, God gave him the recipe for *banh chung,* which uses simple and cheap ingredients. Two of these were made, one round to symbolise the universe and the other square, for the earth. He presented them to the king and, of course, won the throne.

Most families buy or prepare large quantities of *banh chung* a few days before the New Year. They can be served warm or cold, or given as presents, and will keep for a couple of months if not eaten immediately (see Chapter 7, Socialising in Vietnam).

Mooncakes, which are small, sweet, round cakes of Chinese origin, contain a variety of fillings such as red bean paste, lotus seed or an egg yolk mixture. They are eaten during the Mid-Autumn Festival. Sweet rice dumplings with ginger sauce, or *banh troi nuoc,* are eaten on the third day of the third lunar month, during which it is forbidden to light a fire in the kitchen.

EATING OUT

Eating out in Vietnam is cheap, fun and delicious. Good food can be

Outdoor food vendors provide a cheap alternative to restaurants.

enjoyed in a fancy, air-conditioned restaurant or at a street cafe. It is also a way of life in south Vietnam. Few people have a large kitchen, many hold two jobs and wives often work outside the home as well, so many meals are eaten out. In the north where the nights are cooler and the people more careful with their money, restaurants are reserved for special occasions only.

When ordering dishes for the table, it is usual for all dishes to be placed in the centre with people helping themselves to the food, unlike the custom in some other countries where each person orders one dish and eats it himself. The Vietnamese way allows for better balance in a meal. It also allows you to experiment a little in trying out new dishes. As many tastes, textures and colours should be obtained as possible. While it is normal for people to eat the foods in any order, it is preferable to start with the more delicate-tasting dishes and move to the spicier, more robust items. Rice may be brought at the end of the meal but you can ask for it to be brought earlier if you prefer to eat it with the other dishes.

To a foreigner, it can be a little like Russian roulette trying to control the order in which the dishes may appear. Give up, it never works! A foreign travel guide here gives good advice to visiting tourists on how best to order food—just point to the item you want on the menu (do not try to pronounce it), do not ask for a change of ingredients, do not change your order, remember what you ordered (they will not tell you in English when it arrives), accept whatever comes, enjoy it and do not ask for separate bills. This gives you the chance to have a good, hassle-free dinner.

Fastfood is everywhere—not of the type that you get from large franchised stores, but from sellers squatting on every street corner. Most of it is good, wholesome and cheap, but look carefully at the food and the hygiene of the hawkers before buying. Street vendors are very popular and all kinds of food can be bought from them.

Life after work revolves around the street cafes and food. The evenings find many Vietnamese relaxing with a drink in a local cafe. Cafes provide an excellent way to see how the local people live. Endless cups of coffee or tea, or glasses of beer or Coke, are consumed as people chat. Sit for a while and you will usually end up with a few new friends as you swap Vietnamese lessons for English ones.

Many restaurants specialise in certain dishes that are too time-consuming or elaborate to prepare for an ordinary family meal at home. This does not necessarily mean that they are expensive dishes. A filling bowl of *pho* can be bought for less than a dollar. Pancake houses make a popular food called *banh xeo,* which literally means "sound pancake". Its name refers to the noise that the batter makes when it hits the hot griddle. Barbecued dishes are popular and many restaurants let you grill your own meats or seafood on a small cooker that will be brought to your table. This is great fun but can be a hot, smoky experience. Alternatively, order the do-it-yourself dishes that include food and several plates of lettuce leaves, fresh herbs and rice paper. This allows you to wrap a bundle of food, pop it into the dipping sauce and eat your roll. It is somewhat a test of skill to be able to make a bundle that does not disintegrate as you eat it.

If you are vegetarian, there are wonderful restaurants that cater for the Buddhists. Some even produce food that resembles meat so closely that vegetarian "fat" has been put around the outside of a "meat" slice.

Most people enjoy the majority of dishes. But it is wise to know what you are ordering. You will not always get what you expect. For instance, Saigon soup, *hu tieu,* may be served in two separate bowls with the noodles and dry ingredients in one dish and the broth in another. In fact, this soup can be ordered without the broth! That mistake does not seem too bad, but you may be less than pleasantly surprised if you order some of the following dishes by mistake. Dog is commonly eaten in the north of Vietnam and can also be found in the south. Almost all parts of many animals are also consumed, so the swim bladders of fish and the internal organs of fowls and pigs often crop up in dishes. Black chicken, a medicinal dish, has a whole newborn chicken served up in a soup. The sight of it appearing from the broth has been known to test the stomach of many visitors.

Specialty restaurants also exist that sell the meat of exotic animals such as snake, turtle, bear, pangolin, monkey and others. These are usually eaten for their reputed medicinal quality rather than their taste. Foreign business people are often taken there as a show of machismo, a demonstration of status and wealth (they are not cheap) or to show them something unusual. Snake is the most common and it tastes a little like chicken. It is supposed to be rich in protein and calcium but, more importantly, it is said to improve the libido. The animal is usually presented live, then it is killed and the blood is drained off in front of you and presented as a drink. Later, the meat will be prepared separately. If you really cannot handle this, say so when the invitation for dinner is extended to you rather than when you are walking through the restaurant door. In this way, everyone can save face and an alternative restaurant can be chosen.

For the less adventurous, French restaurants, as well as other international cuisines, are found in most larger centres and a wide variety of foodstuffs can now be bought in the cities or found in hotels. Because the Vietnamese start the day early and eat early, restaurants close a little earlier than in most other countries. A late booking can be made around 8–8.30 p.m. Later in the evening, food is always available from street sellers and the larger hotels.

TIPPING

In the past, courtesy was the most important thing to remember when leaving the table. Saying "thank you" still ranks above a tip in some places, although the power of money is making a strong comeback. Service charges are becoming more common, to the extent that one major hotel charges it for takeaway items as well! Do not offer tips if there is already a service charge. If there is no service charge, a tip based on 10% of the bill is the general rule depending, of course, on the quality of service which was extended to you. At times, service is non-existent in any form, in which case you do not need to tip.

CULTURAL QUIZ

Here is a series of situations you may find yourself in. You are bound to encounter many humorous little incidents while living in Vietnam. Sometimes, though, you get to see the funny side only after the event or when it happens to someone else! Check your knowledge of Vietnamese culture and see what you would do or say in such circumstances. The names are fictitious but foreigners have actually encountered similar situations. Sometimes, they are quick enough to find an escape route, but sometimes not! There are no right or wrong answers but some approaches work better than others.

SITUATION 1

You want to open your new office and hold a small function on the first day to celebrate the occasion. You are a little pushed for time as your Canadian headquarters is on your back to open as quickly as possible. You settle on the earliest possible date, which is the day after your return from an important business trip to Singapore. Your staff are unhappy about the date you have chosen but you suspect it is because you are rushing them to get things organised at short notice. Later, you find that not as many people turned up for the welcome drinks as you had hoped. The other foreign companies were well represented but few Vietnamese came. The function was set at five o'clock for cocktails. What went wrong?

A It was the 13th day of the lunar month, which is considered an inauspicious date. You should have checked with your staff first.

B Five o'clock is too early for Vietnamese as they are still at work.

C You sent out the invitations too late and did not give people enough time to rearrange their schedules.

Comments

The time is fine and late invitations are not a problem for the Vietnamese. Very short notice is often given and you may receive an invitation to a function only on the morning itself. Your secretary could easily have followed through with a telephone call, perhaps in the morning, reminding people of the event and saying how pleased you would be if they could attend.

The real problem lies in A. You may not be superstitious but it does not mean your staff and clients are not. The fact that your opening event was poorly attended proves what a bad day it was and future problems will be blamed on it. Get some advice on how to fix the matter.

SITUATION 2

Simon has been in Vietnam for almost a year and has several Vietnamese friends and a Vietnamese girlfriend he is quite keen on. They all speak good English and are part of the young and trendy set. He invites them to join him on Friday night at a popular downtown bar. He is already inside having a drink when his friends arrive as a group. The bar opens into the street and he calls them in. He greets each of them and they stand around for five minutes. Very little is said and when Simon says "Hi" to another friend who has just walked in, the group waves goodbye and leaves.

Where has he gone wrong? They have been out on the town before and spent several hours chatting. He knows they drink alcohol.

A   Simon invited them to a bar that is frequented mainly by foreigners. They felt out of place and embarrassed (that they may not be able to afford the drinks there) and left.

B   He beckoned them in. He should have gone out, welcomed them, invited them in personally, sat them down and bought the drinks. He invited them so he should pay.

C   He was rude to have turned away from them to chat to his new friend who had just walked in. They felt slighted and left.

Comments

Both *A* and *B* are good reasons why they may have left. *B* is particularly true. If you invite people out, you are the host and are expected to greet them properly, settle them down comfortably and pay for all the drinks. *C* is less likely. Everyone has friends and this would not have been seen as impolite as long as Simon did not spend too much time at it.

SITUATION 3

You have just come back from a short trip to Singapore with your wife. There are three secretaries in your office who have been working hard recently, so you decide to bring back a few nice gifts for them. One is married and she and her husband have moved into their own small apartment recently. You decide to bring her back something useful for the house. Your wife buys her some nice casserole dishes. The other two are not married and you buy a copy Chanel handbag for one and a cream scarf for the other because she wears a lot of beige so it should match her outfits.

You have not had time to wrap them so you hand them out when you arrive at the office. The secretaries thank you but do not look overjoyed at the gifts. Why not?

A You bought them different presents and they are trying to work out the value of each to see who received the best deal.

B You did not wrap the presents and display care in the way you handed them out. It implies you do not really think much of them.

C Casserole dishes are not something they can use. Ovens are not common in Vietnam. The Chanel bag is a cheap copy and looks as if it was made locally. The scarf is not much use in the south as it is too warm and no one wears them. It is also the wrong colour.

Comments

They will be trying to work out how much everything costs but that would not have caused them to look glum. You should have wrapped the gifts nicely. No one opens presents in front of the giver but again. that is not cause for the long faces.

C is the correct answer. The scarf was all right but not that useful. Worse still, the colour is unacceptable. It is too close to white and looks like a mourning cloth for a funeral procession. The Chanel bag concept was fine. The people love brand-name products but if you give them a copy, it must be of very good quality so that it still has an imported look. All cooking is done on top of charcoal braziers or on a gas ring. The people do not own ovens but the casserole dishes have lids and can be used as serving dishes, so they are still handy. The secretary who received this is probably the happiest of the three.

SITUATION 4

You have just moved into your new house and there is a knock on the door. The person standing before you is Mr. Lam, a Vietnamese man who lives down the road and speaks some English. He welcomes you, would like to be friends and offers to teach you things about your new neighbourhood and the country. He seems very pleasant and you look forward to his next visit.

On the second visit, he tells you how tough it has been in the last 20 years. He was in the South Vietnamese army and had to go to re-education camp. He still cannot find a good job. He asks to borrow money for a sick son in hospital. On the third visit (just before Tet), he wants to use the telephone to call his sister in the United States. On subsequent visits, he asks for a job, for you to take mail out of the country to be posted or for you to find some foreign friends to whom he can rent his house.

What do you do?

A Give him a small amount of money for his sick son, say that he can use the telephone but must pay for the call and try to set up some job interviews for him (so that you can get him off your back!).

B Look hurt and offended when he asks for money. Tell him you are not a bank and that in your culture, it is very rude for new friends to come begging for money. Make sure he gets the message so that none of his friends come around trying the same trick. Tell your guard not to let him through the gates in future.

C   Offer him a loan at a reasonably high rate of interest and prepare a document covering the terms and repayments. He has to sign this with a Vietnamese third party as witness. The witness could be your joint-venture partner in the government.

D   Apologise for not being able to give any money to his son but offer to accompany him to hospital on his next visit and take some fruit along with you.

Comments

The Vietnamese can be very direct about asking for things and some are not shy in coming forward. It is up to you, but expect to hear quite a few of such tales. Answer A is acceptable, but you may or may not see your money again. He may be in desperate need of money and really have a son in hospital, in which case you have probably found a friend for life. Option D will let you gauge his actual situation, if you have the time to visit.

B is quite offensive. You have been far more rude than was necessary. You could, instead, have made some face-saving excuses if you did not want to help him. C may open a can of worms that you do not want to get into.

There is no point in making enemies of neighbours as they can cause you a great deal of problems if they choose to, such as burglaries and problems with the police. However, do not acquiesce to their requests too much or you will have more people asking for help than you can possibly handle. You are seen as very wealthy. Neighbours watch you move in, buy new furniture, install air-conditioners and go to work every day, dressed nicely. The best option is to try and help him get a job so that he has a source of income. There is a shortage of English speakers so it should not be that hard even if it is just an unskilled job as a security guard with a foreign company.

SITUATION 5

You are just getting started with the company and are negotiating your way through the maze of licensing and approvals. It has taken a long time and approval for the first step has finally come through. To celebrate, you invite a group of officials out to a business dinner. They choose the restaurant and the meal starts well. You enjoy the prawns and beef dishes but when the offal arrives, you are not too happy about it. Anyway, to demonstrate goodwill, you eat a little and are hoping that the meal is about to finish. Then they all start toasting you. You are not a heavy drinker and after a couple of rounds you will probably be a babbling wreck. But the people are very important to you. You cannot afford to get them offside at this stage. What do you do?

A Quietly arrange with the restaurant staff to give you iced tea which is the same colour as the whisky being served.

B Toast the speech made by the first person, drink the whisky but refuse subsequent drinks, saying you are on medication.

C Drink everything down and resign yourself to a rotten hangover the next day.

D Drink a sip with each person but do not swallow the whole lot however strong the protests.

Comments

You could try A. The ploy has worked for at least one foreigner but beware that you do not get caught. Lying to the Vietnamese and being devious in your actions will get you nowhere. You are better off being open about the fact that you are drinking tea and cannot drink alcohol, but that it still boils down to your having a drink with them and enjoying their company. Some people resort to B but it is not ideal. You have drunk with one person but not the rest. When you refuse the second person after obliging the first, you are likely to create some ill feeling. Before the first drink, you should make it clear that you are drinking to everyone. C is possible but you will be expected to repeat the performance the next time around. Solution D is fine.

SITUATION 6

You work in an office comprising five foreigners and eight Vietnamese. Everyone gets on quite well and the group goes out for lunch occasionally. Most of your Vietnamese staff speak good English and are comfortable with foreign ways. In the office, Paul and you are always cracking jokes and teasing each other. It took the staff a little while to get used to that but now that they know you and their English has improved, they laugh at most of it. Mr. Duc, Mrs. Liem and Mr. Nam are jokers themselves and always have a quick comment or will play a little joke themselves. Still, you are quite careful and do not play any of the practical tricks on the Vietnamese. Some of the jokes are a little risque but the ladies giggle as they look away, so you do not feel that you have overstepped the line.

Then one morning, you see Mrs. Liem arriving at work on the back of a young man's new motorcycle. He is certainly not her husband, whom you know quite well. At coffee break in the morning, you tease her about this new man. You make jokes about her new boyfriend and want to know his name. She goes quiet and looks away. Others around you move off. You had expected that they would all join in and be curious. You find out later from Mr. Nam that it was her brother. So what was the problem?

A Her brother is a Viet Kieu who has just come back from Australia. That is why you have not met him before. He is flashing his money around and people are finding it embarrassing. No one wants to talk about it.

B You questioned her propriety. You should never make jokes or insinuate that a Vietnamese woman's morals may be anything but of the highest standard. She is married and must be faithful to her husband. To suggest anything else is a very hurtful and cruel comment.

C You thought it was her boyfriend but it turned out to be her brother. Everyone is embarrassed for you for making such a social gaffe.

Comments

The answer is definitely not *C*. It was a bit of a gaffe but they would simply have told you it was her brother. *A* is a chance, but you are likely to have heard about his impending arrival earlier if you were close to Mrs. Liem. Also, your questions are unlikely to have brought about the reaction that they did. *B* is the major issue. You committed a major sin questioning a woman's morals. Even though you were only joking, you are unlikely to be forgiven easily by Mrs. Liem or the rest of the staff.

SITUATION 7

You arrived two months ago with your wife and daughter. You are getting very tired of having to live in a small hotel room. Thankfully, you have just found a house to rent through your driver, who speaks good English. He conducts all the negotiations with the landlord on your behalf. You have agreed on the price, starting date and renovations, and the landlord's papers are in order. As your company is paying for the rent, the papers will be made out in its name.

You instruct the secretary to type them and then you wait for the necessary approval. After a long while, you find that no progress has been made. When you ask why, everyone blames each other. It has now been a month-and-a-half and the landlord is about to sign the house over to another prospective tenant. Only then do you find out that the cause of the delay lies in the secretary refusing to type the papers without getting her cut on the deal. She played no part in the negotiations and the others do not want to give her the amount she is demanding. What should you do? Do you:

A   Sack her on the spot and use her as an example to your other staff about what you call corruption. She has cost the company an extra six weeks' cost in hotel bills. You threaten to take that out of her salary.

B   Draw her aside and explain that this is not acceptable in a foreign company and force her to prepare the papers right away.

C Ask around and find that similar things happen in other companies. You set out to find out why she is not getting her cut and then
let the whole thing go through.
D Creep in after work and type the letters yourself.
E Get another secretary to do it.

Comments

Well, taking a cut on a deal is a very common practice in Vietnam and
one that is impossible to stamp out completely. What exactly went
wrong will never be known but many deals come unstuck the same
way. The real problem is that it cost the company a lot of extra money
and gave you much heartache.

Option A is what you would love to do but apart from this instance,
her work is acceptable, you are understaffed and the office cannot
afford to lose her at the moment. Option B will not get you anywhere.
She knows that foreign companies do not subscribe to the practice but
that is the way things are in Vietnam! You can make her do the work
immediately. She will probably forego her cut and lose face as well,
but this may cause further problems for you. You can go for C for
expediency, but that commends the sinner and chastises the person
who appeared to be in the right. Option D is impossible unless you can
write Vietnamese fluently, are familiar with protocol and know which
letters go to whom. Option E is a chance, but this secretary may not
know the protocol and have to get advice from the first secretary. You
can bet that cooperation will not be forthcoming from her!

SITUATION 8

You are chatting at the home of a north Vietnamese friend. You get
on well but it is approaching lunchtime so his mother asks if you
would like to join them for the meal. Your friend nods and also
extends the invitation. You do not have anything planned for the next
few hours so you agree. It will be interesting to meet the rest of the
family and see how they eat.

Meal time arrives and you are shown where to sit. Large bowls of food are placed in the centre of the table—rice, a vegetable dish, soup and a fried fish. It smells good and you realise how hungry you are. You are on your best behaviour and wait until the father has started eating. Your friend takes your eating bowl and fills it with rice and adds choice portions from the other dishes. You are busy concentrating on eating with chopsticks and keeping the conversation going. You are not really looking around the table. More food keeps getting added to your bowl and it tastes as good as it smells. You are doing most of the talking, asking questions and being told about Vietnamese customs. Towards the end of the meal, the conversation is getting a little strained and you finally realise that everyone else is eating rice only. They are still very polite to you but their faces are expressionless. What did you do wrong?

A You should have put food in other people's bowls as was done for yours.

B You ate too much without realising that the family did not have sufficient food for an extra mouth.

C   You have monopolised the conversation, talked with your mouth full and asked about customs that they would rather not discuss with a foreigner.

Comments

Option C is not likely to have offended them. The Vietnamese are very proud of their country and customs and are happy to tell a foreigner about themselves. If you ask about a subject they would rather not discuss, they will simply change the topic and ignore your question. Option A is true in that it is polite to show concern for your fellow diners' health and put morsels in their bowls. But this is unlikely to have caused the problem.

The real issue is B. You are in the home of a northerner and the polite thing to do would have been to refuse the invitation in the first place. The invitation was extended to you out of courtesy and you were expected to refuse. They were unprepared and did not have enough food for an extra person. To make matters worse, you ate so much that the other family members had to confine themselves to rice. If you do stay for a meal, eat very little and refuse additional morsels unless there is clearly enough food in the centre for everyone else. The only time it is proper to accept an invitation to a meal at home is when you have been asked several days in advance. Even then, say "Yes" only if the host insists.

SITUATION 9

You sprain your ankle playing tennis. It is not bad but you want to visit a doctor who can tell you the extent of the injury and how long it will be before you can go back to playing tennis. A foreign friend who has lived in Vietnam for several years recommends a local doctor who speaks good English.

You make an appointment, turn up and do not have to wait long before you get to see the doctor. He asks you a few questions. His English is excellent but then he puts his hands on your face and asks whether the ankle is still hurting. You are a little surprised but answer his questions. He continues rubbing different areas of your face harder and harder with different implements. You cannot really see what is going on but you know that your face is hurting. The pain in the ankle seems to subside but you are not sure whether it is because you are now more concerned about the pain on your face. You are relieved when he finally stops. He then sits beside you, asks about your sex life and starts explaining that a healthy sex life will maintain a healthy body. You are both male. What do you do?

A   Walk out screaming that you are not a homosexual.

B   Glance at your watch and declare that you are late for a business meeting and will have to go.

C   Sit and listen and make an appointment to come back with your wife as he suggests.

Comments

The first answer is inappropriate and would offend the doctor and embarrass everyone in the waiting room as well. *B* is acceptable and *C* is all right if you believe in traditional Vietnamese or Eastern forms of healing.

Alternative forms of healing are practised widely in Vietnam and the extent to which the healing is psychologically based is much debated between Asian and Western-trained doctors. Many Asians swear that traditional methods work but it is up to you to decide whether you want to try different remedies. Before you do, however, find out exactly what is to be done as some treatments can cause bruising. If you prefer Western-style medical treatment, choose a Western-trained doctor (they practise in Hanoi, Ho Chi Minh City and Vung Tau) or make it very clear at the beginning that you would only like to receive a Western style of treatment from the doctor.

It is quite normal for your doctor to be concerned about your overall state of health and in Vietnam, this would include your sex life.

SITUATION 10

An important client will be in town for just two days and wants to meet the main people you deal with. You arrange for him to meet officials from the People's Committee and the government, and other business people. It is difficult to work in advance here. You have done your best. Tentative bookings were made two weeks ago, confirmed two days ago, and now that the client is here, your secretary has re-confirmed them. The first two meetings went well and you managed to race from one to the next without much of a hitch.

The next is just after lunch, at 2 p.m. Your secretary calls to say you are on your way and the other secretary confirms the meeting again. You arrive a few minutes late and are asked to wait in the ante-room. It is not air-conditioned and you feel warm. You are served tea. After five minutes, nothing has happened but the secretary smiles and makes an apologetic sign. Another 10 minutes go by. The client is making faces at you. You ask the secretary what is causing the delay and she murmurs and leaves, saying she will check. She does not return. What went wrong and what do you do now?

A   Things are fine. The person you are scheduled to meet is just running late from lunch and you can wait a little longer until you have to head for the next appointment. He could not have forgotten your meeting, it has been confirmed three times.

B   You stick your head around the door and demand to know what is going on. You even ask to meet the vice-president.

C   You have sent three reminders concerning the meeting. He could not have forgotten. You thought all along that you have a good working relationship with him but this must have been deliberate. You storm out, claiming that you have never been treated so rudely in your life. You know that he will come to hear about it.

D   Look for the secretary and explain that you cannot wait any longer as you have another appointment. But you would like to leave the gift and card that you have brought. You know he is very busy and hopefully, things will work out better the next time.

Comments

He will not have forgotten your meeting but may have been called up by a higher official or been delayed in some other way. The secretary is too embarrassed to tell you. She is avoiding you, so you know something has gone wrong. If the second-in-command is there you will get to see him, particularly if you know him. But he has not come out to greet you either. There is a real problem, so option *B* would not necessarily get you far. Option *A* is a possibility but you will just be sitting in the heat making your client less impressed with your skills. Option *C* is to be avoided at all costs if you want to do any business with the person or his company in future. Option *D* will help you in your future dealings. The Vietnamese appreciate doing business with people who understand their problems. You have been polite and saved everyone from embarrassment. He will hear of that and his secretary is very grateful.

SITUATION 11

Your two domestic staff, Chi and Anh, have been with you for nearly eight months. Things have settled down and are going quite smoothly. Their individual duties seem clear and both get along well. They have not taken any holiday during this period. Then you break your leg. You live in a house with four floors. At least, there is a bathroom near your bedroom but the kitchen is two floors away.

Chi responds well. She is always there when you call and goes out of her way to make sure you are comfortable. Anh is also helpful but always seems to appear at the wrong time. She walks into your bedroom without knocking when you are undressing. You end up having to tell her off all the time. Three days later, she says her mother is arriving from the United States the following day for a holiday and she will have to take three weeks off.

A This is just a ploy to get out of the extra work while you are in a cast and you sack Anh on the spot.

B Anh is annoyed with you for telling her off and this is her revenge.

Perhaps she is going to look for another job.

C Anh's mother is really coming over. She did not want to tell you earlier as you had looked so unhappy all the time and she did not want to make you feel worse.

Comments

The Vietnamese are not so lazy that they will not get on with extra work, so option *A* is less likely. Option *B* is possible if you have been quite rude to her. Option *C* is most likely. People will avoid telling you something for as long as possible, knowing the news will upset you. Your logic may tell you to give the person as much warning as possible so they can make other arrangements but the Vietnamese do not reason things out that way. Since you have broken your leg, it is even harder for Anh to tell you that she needs time off as she knows you need the extra help around the house.

SITUATION 12

Marjorie and Tom are an older couple who have been in Vietnam for two years. They like the country and its people. It shows even though they have not learned much of the language. Tom works for a large company and has offered Miss Tan a job. However, Miss Tan, who is well-educated and speaks good English, has received a better job offer elsewhere and has accepted it. Now, she visits their house almost every week or two to chat, bringing a small gift each time. To begin with, Marjorie and Tom were happy to see her on their doorstep, despite the fact that she always arrives unannounced and the timing, usually on Saturday afternoons, is not always convenient. She is very pleasant and has taught them many things about Vietnam. They are happy with her visits but just wish they were planned. Now, the continual stream of small presents is starting to embarrass them. What should they do?

A When Miss Tan is about to leave and asks if she may visit again, Marjorie and Tom should say they are very busy over the next few weeks. Perhaps she can telephone first and check.

B Offer to visit her the next time around. Wait for a few weeks, then take a small (perhaps imported) present along.

C Plan to be out for the next few Saturday afternoons without telling her and see what happens.

D Try to get Miss Tan to agree to come at a certain time the following week.

Comments

Miss Tan is being friendly and it is customary in Vietnam to bring small gifts for a friend when you visit the house. Because Marjorie and Tom always welcome her, sit her down, open some imported biscuits or provide nibbles and treat her well, she is flattered and enjoys being their friend. She is learning more about their country and polishing her English too. She feels she should bring a token of her thanks in return.

Any of the options will help encourage her to telephone first. She visits when she has some spare time and few Vietnamese use a diary and book things a week or two in advance. Option *D* may not work for this reason. She may shake her head and not be able to commit herself in advance. Option *A* is good. Emphasise that you would like her to visit again, but when you are free, so she does not think that you do not welcome her. You can try option *B* but she would much prefer to visit you. She may be embarrassed that her house is so small. Option *C* may backfire and encourage her to visit at an even less suitable time than Saturday afternoons!

SITUATION 13

Bob returns from a meeting and his secretary, Trinh, bursts into tears. Her voice is hoarse and he cannot understand what she is saying. Something has happened in her family. He reaches for a box of tissues and hands it to her, putting his arm around her in a comforting manner. Trinh freezes and races for the door. She brushes past Huong, whose face resembles a wooden mask.

Bob races out to Huong and asks her to go and comfort Trinh because she is crying and he does not know what is wrong. They are gone for some time and he returns to his work. When Huong returns, Bob goes to check. She will not look him in the eye but mumbles that it has something to do with Trinh's brother. Bob explains his concern and his actions—why he put his arm around her. Huong relaxes and says "yes", she understands. Trinh returns the next day. Bob does not make a fuss about her absence and work continues as usual.

Three days later, an official from the Ministry of Labour visits and tells Bob that he has been accused of seriously mistreating his employees, taking advantage of his position as supervisor and making sexual advances towards his staff. Bob is horrified. What does he do?

A   Talk to the official in the presence of Trinh and Huong and tell what really happened.

B   Pull a bottle of whisky out of his bottom drawer and explain what had happened, hoping that the official will realise the mistake.

C   Tell the official he has a wife and two lovely sons at home and how dare he come into the office and make accusations about Bob's fidelity—as if he would try it on a Vietnamese secretary.

D   Send out a memo explaining his actions, apologising for his behaviour and for any misunderstanding that has occurred.

Comments

Option *A* would be good but is highly unlikely to work. Neither girl is likely to say anything. If Bob forces them to speak up, their statements would appear to have been coerced. This may not help as Huong may not have believed his explanation. Her "yes" simply indicated that she understood him, not that she agreed with what he was telling her. Option *B* will be seen for the direct bribe that it is. Option *C* will not work and will make the official even more suspicious. After all, some foreigners do cheat on their wives and many Vietnamese men have a mistress.

Option *D* may be the best bet, if Bob had resorted to it earlier. The Vietnamese are extremely sensitive about physical contact between men and women and about the influence of foreigners in their country. Once the matter has been taken up with the Ministry of Labour, it is hard to resolve without causing lasting problems.

RESOURCES

GOVERNMENT STRUCTURE

National

Vietnam is governed according to its 1992 Constitution—as a socialist state under the leadership of the Vietnam Communist Party. However, the ruling bodies of Vietnam are quite convoluted in structure and have changed slightly, and it can be quite difficult to understand what power lies where. There are three groupings:

1. Only one political party is permitted. Leading the country is the secretary-general of the Communist Party. The party plays a very active role in daily life and is at least as important as its elected officials. Chapter meetings are held at the local level to ensure that the party's views are carried out in factories, schools and at all levels of society. A National Congress of Delegates elects the Party Central Committee, which in turn elects an executive from which the Politburo, party secretary-general and secretariat are chosen.

   The party secretary-general chairs the Politburo. It directs the work of the ministries, initiates laws for the National Assembly to ratify, and has the power to pass ordinances when the National Assembly is in recess.

2. The National Assembly has 395 members who are elected every five years by citizens over the age of 18. It meets twice a year and is the only group with the power to pass legislation. It is usually seen as providing the rubber stamp on Politburo and government decisions.

3. Each government department is headed by a minister. The ministers collectively form the Cabinet. Together with the prime minister, vice-premiers and others of equivalent status, they form the government. The group runs the country and reports to the National Assembly. The government is the highest administrative body in the country and it drafts laws and other bills for the National Assembly to consider. It can issue decrees regarding the implementation of an existing law or, if there is no relevant law, it may issue a decree (without the force of law) until new legislation is passed which supersedes it.

There are 19 ministers and ministries and each issues circulars and regulations concerning their area. Special standing committees have been established to cover certain areas such as the State Committee for Cooperation and Investment, State Committee for Planning, State Committee for Inspection, State Committee for Prices, State Bank and State Committee for Science, Technology and the Environment. PetroVietnam, the regulating body for the petroleum industry, has a similar status.

Government Structure—Local

At the local government level, each province elects a People's Committee which has authority over that area. It, in turn, elects an Executive People's Committee of only a few people who carry out the running of the area on a day-to-day basis. It is not essential that a person must belong to the Communist Party to become an elected member of these committees.

Bureaucracy can be slow-moving as there are 40 provinces, plus one special zone (Vung Tau) and three municipalities (Ho Chi Minh City, Hanoi and Haiphong). Each of these is then divided into municipalities, towns, districts and villages.

Complications

The structure seems to work quite well at the national level as well as the National Assembly, Party Central Committee and Politburo levels. The prime minister's office and the various ministries also work well together. When the three parallel political structures are extended down to the district level, the People's Committee has a great deal more power than the other two.

Complications can and do arise as the district and provincial authorities and administrative officers do not feel bound to simply implement the nationally decided policies. Instead, they "interpret" the policies from Hanoi in a way that suits their province and there are often marked discrepancies from area to area. So what is acceptable in one province may not get approval in another. The national government has no direct control over the provincial administrators as they are elected in a decentralised manner by local party members.

This can be very positive and there is plenty of evidence suggesting that *Doi Moi* (the economic reforms of the 1980s) arose as a result of many local changes in that direction. It can also be very negative and your company may have gone through all the right channels and obtained national approval, but the whole process must be repeated at the local level. Numerous businesses have been stalled because they obtained permission from one and not the other. Negotiate with both parties. Keep all officials informed. Do not assume that approval from one will automatically get you approval from the other.

BUSINESS AND INVESTMENT RESOURCES

Foreign investment rules are changing rapidly as the needs of Vietnam and foreign investors become clearer. This also applies to banking, legal implications, taxation and other policies. There are a number of sources for up-to-date information. It is easy to get incorrect information so make sure that you check and re-check everything.

Books and brochures on foreign business and investment become out of date as soon as they are printed. Banks, accounting firms or legal offices are some of the best sources for quality information.

Companies such as Deloitte Touche Tohmatsu International, Freehill Hollingdale & Page, Baker and McKenzie, Ernst & Young, KPMG Peat Marwick, Sly and Weigall, Coopers & Lybrand, Price Waterhouse, Maddock Lonie & Chisholm, Blake Dawson Waldron and Phillips Fox, together with the State Committee for Cooperation and Investment in Vietnam, have printed brochures or booklets designed for business people and investors.

A sample of additional materials are:

- *A Legal Handbook for Foreign Investors in Vietnam* by Le Thanh Chan, The Gioi Publisher, 1994. This is part of a series which includes special guides for groups such as the Viet Kieu, among others.
- *Vietnam: A Guide to the Legal Framework* by Clifford Chance, 1994.
- *Vietnam: The New Investment Frontier* by Phillip Donald Grub and Nguyen Xuan Oanh, 1992, HCMC Publishing House.

There is a wide range of UNDP and World Bank papers available, together with books from various Vietnamese government agencies. Photocopies of these are on sale in many bookshops. So are photocopies of other works but these are sometimes doctored and their information and statistics may not be reliable.

Export Processing Zones

Note that the foreign investment guidelines are different if your business has been set up within one of the Export Processing Zones. Tax savings are available as all goods produced within these are destined for overseas markets. There are also other variations in the terms and conditions that generally apply to companies operating within Vietnam. There are five export processing zones: two in Ho Chi Minh City, and one each in Can Tho, Haiphong and Da Nang. Only one is currently operational and that is the Tan Thuan Export Processing Zone in Ho Chi Minh City.

USEFUL ADDRESSES

Schools
International Grammar School
236 Nam Ky Khoi Nghia Street, Q3
Ho Chi Minh City
Tel: 223337, 293237, fax: 230000
(This is an English-language school that caters for kindergarten to grade 10 levels.)

L'Ecole Collette
124 Cach Mang Thang 8
Ho Chi Minh City
Tel: 291992
(A French school catering for children from 3 to 16 years old.)

United Nations International School
c/o U.N.D.P. Hanoi
Box 618, Bangkok
Thailand 10501

Hanoi-Amsterdam School
Giang Vo
Tel: 263635 (Hanoi number), fax: 263635
(An English-language school for children aged between 4 and 14, ranging from pre-kindergarten to grade 8. The second languages taught are French, Swedish and Vietnamese.)

Ecole Francaise International De Hanoi
Hanoi-Amsterdam School
Giang Vo
Tel: 232023, fax: 232023
(French-speaking classes for pre-kindergarten to higher secondary levels.)

The Russian School
56/58 Pho Nguyen Thai Hoc
Tel: 252170
(Secondary school classes in Russian. Foreigners are provided with
a Russian-language course.)

The Finnish School
Hanoi Water Supply Project
Mai Dich
Tel: 344039
(Primary and secondary school classes in Finnish.)

ENGLISH-LANGUAGE PUBLICATIONS

Currently, there is a proliferation of newspapers and magazines to
help the reader keep in contact with happenings in Vietnam. These
can easily be found in major hotels, or on sale in the streets of the
larger cities. None give good overseas coverage and most people rely
on satellite television or short-wave radio to keep up to date on these
matters. Foreign publications, particularly the Asian-oriented ones,

can be purchased. They include the *International Herald Tribune*, *Bangkok Post*, *Far Eastern Economic Review*, *Newsweek* and *Times*.

A limited number of other publications, covering mostly fashion or sports, can also be found. These tend to be very expensive and most people bring them in themselves when they return from overseas trips. Very few novels are available in the shops, although major hotels stock some. Photocopied versions of books on Vietnam can be purchased from small shopkeepers, but these are considered illegal.

LOCAL PRODUCTIONS IN ENGLISH

Vietnam Today, a monthly colour magazine
Vietnam Economic Times, a monthly colour magazine
Vietnam Investment Review, a weekly paper, available in both English and Vietnamese versions
Vietnam Economic Times, a monthly magazine
Vietnam News, daily four-page newspaper
Vietnam Courier, a weekly

FLAG

Vietnam's flag is red with a gold star in its centre. This symbol is incorporated into many signs and advertisements in a show of patriotism. The red background is in memory of the lives lost in Vietnam's move towards independence. The star is there to lead people forward into the future.

THE NATIONAL ANTHEM

Tien Quan Ca (Marching to the Front) is the song used to call the Vietnamese forward to fight for independence. It was adopted by the northern soldiers during the Vietnam War and is still sung today.

HEALTH

First-Aid Kit

Bring your preferred medicines. Items that may be quite difficult to obtain in Vietnam include gauzes, bandages, dressings, scissors, disposable scalpels and pincers. Other things you may need soon after you arrive are antiseptics, insect repellent. paracetamol (Panadol), immodium, antacid and water-sterilising tablets (if you intend travelling off the beaten path). Most people arrive with the necessary medication and more is better than less when you are in Vietnam. Watch out for expiry dates and take care not to store things in a warm place, which will limit their shelf life.

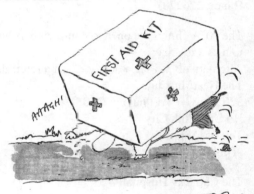

Medical Contacts

Ho Chi Minh City:
OSCAT/AEA International Clinic
Han Nam Building
65 Nguyen Du Street, Q1
Ho Chi Minh City
Tel: 298520, fax: 298551
(This is a 24-hour alarm centre for evacuations as well as a clinic for medical assistance. It can provide consultation, X-rays, ultrasound scanning as well as pharmacy, dental and laboratory services.)

253

The organisation also operates a clinic in Vung Tau. The address is:
OSCAT/AEA International
1 Duong Than Thai
Vung Tau
Tel: 64-58776, fax: 64-58779

International SOS (For evacuations or medical assistance)
151 Vo Thi Sau Street, Q3
Ho Chi Minh City
Tel: 294386, fax: 242862
(24-hour emergency alarm numbers:
Ho Chi Minh City: 242866, 294386, 242864)
Hanoi: 226228)

The AEA clinics are open to non-members but you may be asked to join as a member.
Alternatively, to see a doctor or get a referral, you can call:
The Heart Institute
520 Nguyen Tri Phuong, Q10
Ho Chi Minh City
Tel: 651586
(This is a well-run clinic and foreign doctors are available.)

The Cho Ray Hospital
210B Nguyen Chi Thanh Street, Q5
Ho Chi Minh City
Tel: 554137/8, 558794, 558863

If you are a European Union expatriate, try:
The French Consulate
27 Xo Viet Nghe Tinh Street
Ho Chi Minh City
Tel: 297231
(Open Monday–Friday, 8 a.m.–12 noon and 2–5.30 p.m.)

Pharmacies

Many exist, some attached to clinics or hospitals. A well-patronised
pharmacy where the staff speak both English and French is:
199 Hai Ba Trung Street, Q3
Ho Chi Minh City

In Hanoi, there are:

The Swedish Clinic
358 Khu Ba Dinh/Van Phuc (opposite the Swedish Embassy)
Tel: 252464
(Open: Monday and Friday, 9–11.30 a.m. and 1.30–4.30 p.m., Tues-
day to Thursday, 1.30–4.30 p.m. The clinic deals with outpatients
only but can dispense vaccines and most medication. It will also make
dental and paediatric referrals.)

Bac Mai Hospital
Giai Phong Street
Tel: 522089 (International Department)
Tel: 57088 (for tropical and infectious diseases)
Tel: 257011, 253731 ext. 20 (for cardiac problems)

The Institute of Opthalmology
85 Ba Trieu Street
Tel: 263966/7, 226125/6

Dr. Le Trinh
16B Han Thuyen Street
Tel: 254946
(This woman doctor practises traditional medicine, acupuncture and
physical therapy. She also makes home visits.)

AEA International:
(A 24-hour alarm centre with an expatriate nurse, paramedic and doctor in attendance)
4 Tran Hung Dao
Hanoi
Tel: 213555, fax: 213523

International SOS
60 Nguyen Du, Suite 208
Tel: 226228, fax: 269166

BIBLIOGRAPHY

Travel Books

Cohen, Barbara, *The Vietnam Guide Book*, Houghton Mifflin Company, Massachusetts, USA, 1991. Comprehensive but sections are a little dated.

Hiebert, Murray, *Vietnam Notebook—Vietnam, A Survivor's Guide for Serious Investors, Intrepid Tourists and Curious Observers*, Review Publishing Company, 1993. A well-researched series of snippets on different aspects of Vietnamese life.

Nepote, Jacques and Guillaume, Xavier, *Odyssey Illustrated Guide to Vietnam*, Odyssey, 1992. An informative guide looking at some cultural and historic aspects.

West, Helen (ed.), *Vietnam*, Insight Guides, 1992.

Historical Accounts

Evans, Grant and Rowley, Kelvin, *Red Brotherhood at War— Vietnam, Cambodia and Laos since 1975*, Verso, 1990. A thorough examination of the politics of the period.

Hayslip, Le Ly, *When Heaven and Earth Changed Places*, Pan Books, London, 1994. Also a movie, this book looks at the difficulties faced by Vietnamese in the north and south during the Vietnam War and in its aftermath.

Kemf, Elizabeth, *Month of Pure Light—The Re-Greening of Vietnam*, The Women's Press, 1990. During a series of visits to the country, the author tries to examine the extent of environmental degradation still existing from the Vietnam War and the impact it has had on the people. Tied up with this are her perceptions of the people and an account of the personal traumas she has suffered.

Lewis, Norman, *A Dragon Apparent—Travels in Cambodia, Laos and Vietnam*, Eland, London 1982. An excellent book revealing many aspects of Vietnam as it was in the 1800s when the author travelled through the region.

Ninh, Bao, *The Sorrow of War*, Secker and Warburg, UK, 1993. This novel, written by a respected North Vietnamese soldier, does not glorify the communist victory but looks at the terrible toll exacted on the people.

Palmos, Frank, *Ridding the Devils*, Bantam, 1990. A former war journalist revisits Vietnam and looks for a North Vietnamese soldier who almost killed him. A well-written book.

Wintle, Justin, *The Vietnam Wars—Wars of the Modern Era*, Weidenfeld and Nicolson, London, 1991. An easy-to-read summary.

Language

Nguyen Anh Que, *Vietnamese for Foreigners*, Hanoi 1994.

Nguyen Van Khon, *Vietnamese for You*, Nha Xuat Ban Tre, 1992.

Vietnamese Phrase Book, Lonely Planet publications, Victoria, Australia, 1993.

Foods

Ngo, Bach and Zimmerman, Gloria, *The Classic Cuisine of Vietnam*, Penguin 1986.

Routhier, Nicole, *The Foods of Vietnam*, 1989, Stewart, Tabori and Chang, NY.

General

Bakaert, Jacques and Hall, Tim, *Vietnam: A Portrait*, Elsworth Books Ltd, Hong Kong, 1993. A pictorial guide to the country.

Butler, Robert Olen, *A Good Scent from A Strange Mountain*, Minerva, 1993. A selection of well-written, easy-to-read stories providing insights into the people's way of thinking.

Crawford, Ann Caddwell, *Customs and Culture in Vietnam*, Charles E. Tuttle Co. Publishers, Rutland, Vermont and Tokyo, Japan.

Nguyen Trong Dieu, *Geography of Vietnam*, The Gioi Publishers, 1992.

Wintle, Justin, *Romancing Vietnam*, Penguin, UK, 199_.

Others

There are many locally produced books covering specific areas you may be interested in such as Vietnamese Buddhism, water puppets or traditional medicine.

THE AUTHOR

Claire Ellis was born in Scotland, brought up in Australia, lived in the United States and now resides and travels in Southeast Asia. Because of her husband's career, she has regularly shifted from country to country. Each time, she starts anew the process of learning about a new place as well as settling down and making a home. Through these moves, she has developed a keen interest in the cultural differences and nuances both between and within countries in the region.

Claire, who is a qualified teacher, has a degree in Economics and honours in Urban Geography. The constant moving has encouraged her to focus on writing. She moved to Vietnam in 1993 and was based in Ho Chi Minh City but also travelled widely, working as a freelance journalist contributing mostly to business and travel magazines.

In 1995, after living in Vietnam for more than a year, Claire and her husband moved again, this time to set up home in Jakarta, Indonesia.

INDEX